The Winds of Promise

The Winds of Promise

Building and Maintaining Strong Clergy Families

Anne E. Streaty Wimberly
and
Edward P. Wimberly

DISCIPLESHIP RESOURCES

PO BOX 340003 • NASHVILLE, TN 37203-0003
www.discipleshipresources.org

Cover design by Shawn Lancaster.
Interior design by PerfecType, Nashville, TN.

ISBN: 978-0-88177-496-2

Library of Congress Control Number 2007922195

For information regarding rights and permissions, contact Discipleship
Resources, PO Box 340003, Nashville TN 37203-0003; fax 615-340-1789.

Discipleship Resources®, and design logos are trademarks owned by
GBOD®, Nashville, Tennessee. All rights reserved.

In honor of
Clergy Families who seek the
winds of promise and testify
to their presence.

CONTENTS

FOREWORD

In freshman English class my son's teacher asked if anyone in the group was a "PK"—preacher's kid. He raised his hand then realized he was the only one in this class. Later that day when I picked him up from school, we had a brief discussion about how he feels when people refer to him as a "PK."

Our church has a concern for all who are preacher's kids; for all who are spouses of clergy; and for all clergy seeking to live faithfully in response to their call as clergy and additionally in response to their call to live faithfully within family. We find this concern addressed particularly in The United Methodist Church through two particular resolutions adopted at the 2004 General Conference: "Support of Clergy Families" and "Caring for Clergy Spouses, Children, and Youth During Divorce."

We are not alone. The Episcopal Church has the organization, "Families of Clergy United in Support (FOCUS, Inc.), specifically for aiding clergy families. Other denominations share concern about the health and strength of clergy families as well.

What are factors that place clergy families at risk? One strain felt by all is summed up in the phrase, "Called by God." That's what any of us feel who are ordained as clergy in the church. This calling shapes our work, our vision of life, our participation in the community, and our families. I read with interest the quote included in *The Winds of Promise* from a teenage girl who stated to her clergy parent, "You were called to ministry. I wasn't." She then went on to talk about how congregations extend the expectation of call to spouses and children in clergy families. This is just one of the challenges Ed and Anne Wimberly address in their book, *The Winds of Promise*.

Outlined in *The Winds of Promise* are these challenges felt by clergy families: meeting expectations of a congregation; moving; making family life count; meaning-making in parsonage living; managing catastrophic events and other devastating circumstances. Each is framed by the stories of Ed and Anne and by the stories they have been told through years of working with clergy families.

However, if Ed and Anne only outlined the challenges, we would all feel cheated because knowing them isn't enough. Having a methodology for addressing them is what clergy families need. Ed and Anne provide a workable methodology for individuals, couples, and children in clergy families to explore the issue, tell the stories, and build individual and family strength to withstand the stress. I was intrigued by the concept of "spiritual elasticity" for becoming resilient and strong as individuals and as family. Ed and Anne do not minimize the force of the stress. They don't pretend that these challenges will go away. Instead, they acknowledge how hurtful and debilitating each of the challenges can be, and through the story-sharing process, help those in families develop the elasticity needed to face the challenges.

I am hopeful that clergy families will read and use *The Winds of Promise*. I am also hopeful that those in congregations will also read this asking first, "Where can we be more realistic in our demands on clergy families?" and second, "What of this method can we use in our families to build strength and increase our faith?"

—MaryJane Pierce Norton
Team Leader for Family, Life Span, & Latino Ministries
General Board of Discipleship of the United Methodist Church

PREFACE

This is a book about the lives of clergy families. Most importantly, it tells and invites the stories of clergy families that often go untold, especially the stories of struggle. Our constant question along the way has been: "Is it really important that the stories be told?" The answer that has come not simply from within us but from countless others is a resounding "Yes!"

We confess that the writing of the book invited us into very moving experiences of our own recall and story-sharing. Each of us was part of a clergy family during our formative years, and we became a clergy family when we married. Thus, in our writing, we felt compelled to share parts of our journey. Our own stories, and the stories shared with us by many, many others, affirm that clergy family life unfolds with heart warming experiences of accomplishment, affirmation, and reward. This truth cannot be overestimated. But, heart tugging challenges that touch clergy family life can become gale-force winds not always easily faced. Among the most notable of these challenges is moving, meeting expectations, making family life count, and meaning-making in parsonage "glass-house" living. Moreover, clergy families are not exempt from heart-wrenching pain associated with managing catastrophic events and devastating circumstances. Where do we go to tell the truth about these struggles? Are there occasions for truth-telling that hold promise of release and relief?

Often the tendency on the part of clergy and family members is to endure challenge in silence, either for fear of complaining, or because there is no place or time to translate into words the realities of everyday life. But, there is something of inestimable value and importance in telling the stories. For this reason, the book centers on the key activity of story-telling.

The book builds on our own experiences and years of conversations with clergy families in workshops and retreats we have led, and through a variety of other leadership opportunities carried out within denominational, congregational, and seminary settings. Our underlying premise is that story-sharing opens the way for cathartic moments for us to release concerns of the heart and honest feelings about very personal happenings along the sojourn in and beyond congregational life. It invites the lament, which is the voice of pain, and prayer, which opens the way to promise. Story-sharing in the presence of others also creates opportunity for forming relationships where support, empathy, and understanding reside. We gain clarity about key issues needing attention and about used and unused resilience in the form of resources of self as well as of others alongside God's enabling presence and activity. We further contend that, through story-sharing, we discover or rediscover the necessity, the courage, and the kinds of action needed to continue on. Story-sharing fosters our discernment and experience of the winds of promise.

We invite clergy family members into story-sharing and reflection through a step-by-step process. Our goal is to assist family members in uncovering challenges, exploring resilience, deciding ways of building and drawing on resiliency, and experiencing the renewing breath of God or God's *ruach*. Families may enter into story-sharing alone or in small groups. However, spiritual guides, other care-giving professionals, and denominational leaders may use this book to organize and lead clergy family groups, retreats, or workshops.

Apart from our own, the stories and situations of numerous pastors and families introduce key themes in clergy families' experiences of struggle and give evidence of the winds of promise. In actuality, we owe a tremendous debt of gratitude to literally hundreds upon hundreds of colleagues, workshop and retreat participants, close friends, and students across the years whose stories have helped shape the book. Although there are far too many to name them all individually, there are among them special ones that must be mentioned. We remember with heartfelt appreciation the journeys and lessons learned from our parents, the late Reverend Robert H. Streaty and Mrs. Valeska Streaty, and the late Reverend Edgar V. Wimberly, Sr. and Mrs. Evelyn P. Wimberly. Added to our parents are our siblings, including Roberta J. Streaty Towell, Robert Streaty, Jr., Reverend Joseph Michael Streaty, Jon A. Streaty, Pamela Wimberly Jones, and the late Edgar V. Wimberly, Jr.

During our early experience as a clergy family forty years ago, we also recall with thanks small clergy groups with whom the importance and vitality of story-sharing were unmistakable. One close-knit group included Reverend Joseph Bassett and Mrs. Nancy Bassett, and Reverend Cameron Borton and Mrs. Joan Borton. Another group included Reverend Dr. Archie Smith and Mrs. Jerry Smith, and Reverend Richard Campbell and Mrs. Laura Campbell. A third couple-to-couple story-sharing relationship was with Reverend John Parker and Mrs. Kathy Parker.

Over a lengthy span of years, we have been touched by the stories of pastors and their families shared in a variety of workshops, retreats, classes, and other small and large group settings. We recall here with gratitude participants in these settings, particularly those in Central Illinois, East Ohio, Louisiana, Missouri East, North Georgia, and West Michigan Annual Conferences of The United Methodist Church; Black clergy from the North and South Indiana Annual Conferences of The United Methodist Church and the Memphis Annual Conferences Ethnic Local Church Summit; the State of the Black Family meeting sponsored by the African American Episcopal (AME) Church in South Carolina; Clergy families in Louisiana and Mississippi in the Christian Methodist (CME) Church; and pastors in the Zimbabwe Africa Annual Conference. We are grateful as well for the more than one hundred pastors and their families who attended a retreat for those affected by hurricanes Katrina and Rita in 2006. Insights have also come from meetings at Gettysburg Lutheran Theological Seminary; the Memphis Theological Seminary; Lancaster Theological Seminary; Moravian Theological Seminary; The United Methodist Church General Board of Discipleship Convocation for Pastors of African American Churches; and ones carried out in conjunction with the Faith and Health Program of Interdenominational Theological Center (ITC).

No book comes to completion without the technical, close reading, and editing skills of others. We are immensely grateful to Ms. Cassandra Dorsey and Reverend Richelle White for these special gifts.

Toward the Winds of Promise: A Starting Point

People are like plants in the wind: they
bow down and rise up again.
—A MALAGASY PROVERB ON RESILIENCE[1]

Recalling Our Story

Over the years, we have had many opportunities to reflect on our unfolding stories from the time we were children in clergy families—or preacher's kids, as we were called—to and beyond our experience of becoming a couple in parish ministry. During and after our courtship and marriage, we have spoken of successes attained by our clergy fathers' leadership, our mothers' efforts, the members' ideas and competence, and of expectations for us to contribute our time and talents on behalf of the ministry. But, we also reminisced about our parents' experiences of struggle along the way, their dashed hopes for positive ministry outcomes, meager income, illness of family members, and pressure on us to be exemplary preacher's kids. And, we remembered the seemingly endless responsibility for the lives of others that appeared as a given for both of our parents.

The journey we recall from our vantage point as children in clergy families was clearly one of contrasts—times of promise and fulfillment and occasions of deep pain and challenge. Honestly, sometimes the latter seemed to overwhelm the former. Moreover, each family member responded to clergy family life in a uniquely personal way. Each of us struggled in our own way with moving from established friend networks, adapting to new environments and opportunities, and being placed and treated as central figures in congregational life. Every family member did not embrace change and the demands of congregational life easily or with resolve. Clearly, all of us saw and felt keenly the triumphs and woes of family and church.

The realities of our families' journeys in ministry were etched in our memories when we married and entered parish ministry. Frankly, in light of the struggles, we recalled the great concern of Ed's mom about his movement toward pastoral ministry and Anne's intent not to marry a minister. Nonetheless, we knew God had called us together in marriage and to the same ministry trajectory as our parents.

As we look back, we have discovered some insights on the nature of resilience along the journey conveyed by our parents. Several images come to mind. First, there was always time for story, most especially around the meal table. Even though concrete solutions to issues raised were not always approached or revealed, the opportunity for each of us as family members to tell something of our day-to-day story was freeing. Sharing in this manner and being heard made a major difference in our lives.

Second, in Anne's family, singing the songs of Zion was a ritual of encouragement and survival. The message of songs was a way of unpacking our stories and gleaning a way forward. In times of distress, mother could be heard singing the lament, "Sometimes I feel like a motherless child a long way from home," and Daddy would sing, "When the storms of life are raging, God, stand by me," and the words of the hymn, "On Christ the solid rock I stand, all other ground is sinking sand." The piano was also the gathering place for the family's unified voice in songs, such as "Walk together children, don't you get weary," "I've come this far by faith leaning on the Lord," "I don't feel no ways tired; I've come too far from where I started from. Nobody told me the road would be easy. I don't believe God brought me this far to leave me," and "I'm gonna trust in the Lord."

Third, the necessity and profundity of family prayer was a constant in both of our families. The words of Ed's dad have remained an especially powerful example of a way of nurturing resilience: "God, prop us up on every leaning side, and give us always a vision of your will for our lives; and may we cooperate with what you are doing in our lives to make and keep us whole."

In addition to these three images, there was also a rich biblical story-telling environment within our homes. We both learned to allow biblical stories to form and shape our lives, and we never have abandoned that tradition. In fact, drawing on biblical stories has not only been a source of inspiration, but it has also helped us develop the capacity to draw on biblical plots to lean into life in creative and imaginative ways. In other words, identifying with plots was our way of developing a capacity for imagination and novelty, which became keys in learning to be resilient in the face of the demands of being members of clergy families.

Finally, our families emphasized the liberating role of education. Being African Americans, our parents always emphasized that education had the power to enable us to transcend the meanness of life and to find a Christian vocation that could bring meaning in our lives. From our faith as well as an education, we were taught that we could live creative and meaningful lives despite the circumstances that life presented us.

In our journey forward as a clergy couple, we have recognized the significance of story-sharing, family ritual and prayer, and education as pivotal pathways to resilience, especially in times of challenge. Indeed, the imperative call for resilience became highlighted in our moves from one place to another, the challenge of ministry in divergent contexts amidst the death of one child two days after birth and the loss of three others by miscarriage, plus concerns for aging parents. Sharing with other clergy couples and engaging in our own times of ritual and prayer became vital means by which we envisioned and embraced the way forward in our lives.

Awareness of Others' Stories

Over time, we have discovered that there is a profound need of clergy families in general, to voice especially their stories of challenge and pain. More than this, our workshops with clergy families, work with seminarians, and other personal contacts with clergy families have revealed the importance of focusing on how to build and maintain inner resilience and strength to continue their lives. The critical nature of the need was powerfully demonstrated in a long distance call we received sometime ago from a clergy friend who sought prayer for strength in the midst of a family crisis, exacerbated by relocation to a new congregation. During the week of transition from one church to the other, the clergyman's pregnant wife was diagnosed with diabetes and underwent emergency

delivery by caesarean section. The mother was hospitalized in the local-
ity of the former church for post-delivery and diabetic treatment, while
the premature infant was rushed to another hospital for neonatal care.
Relatives in still another town took the couple's other children. The pastor completed packing and overseeing the movement of the family's
belongings in order to make way for the incoming clergy family.

In maintaining contact with the pastor, we learned about his great
concern that, even though he had kept in telephone contact, visits with
his wife had been limited. He said that his wife told of her concern for
all that needed to be done in the throes of moving. In an apologetic tone,
the pastor still spoke of praying that she understood. Before the dis-
charge of his wife, he had also received a call indicating that the newborn baby was well enough to be released from the hospital. The pastor
was able to negotiate with the hospital to keep the baby until his wife
could be discharged. He was concerned about the other children, especially the oldest who was having tremendous difficulty with the move
away from a revered peer group and community in which he had built
a comfort zone. The pastor spoke of having a meeting at the new church
and a sermon to finish and deliver during the upcoming Sunday service.
He kept saying, "I don't want to get off on the wrong foot. I've got to get
through this, and I know I can with God's help. I've just got to keep
going."

In a subsequent call, the pastor's wife answered the phone. She had
been released from the hospital under orders of restricted activity, but
was caring for the newborn as best she could. The other children were
expected within the week. Both she and her clergy spouse were grateful
that some of the members of the new congregation had offered help.
However, they felt that they didn't want to appear as a burden, since
they were so new to the church. They felt it was important not to rely
much on them. Through her tears, the pastor's wife said, "I feel so guilty
that I'm not able to help more with all that needs to be done to get settled into this new church. I'm thinking, too, about what the new church
is expecting of me and how I'm going to handle things with the children.
Plus, I didn't want to move. I wasn't ready to move. But, I have to believe
that we're going to make it somehow. We've been through a lot of things
before now and I believe we'll come through this time. To tell you the
truth, though, it's not easy. No, it's not easy."

In our recall of this family, our minds also turned to an annual conference retirement celebration during which each retiring pastor spoke.

We remember vividly the words of one of these pastors. The words went something like this: "I have itinerated for thirty-five years. And, now, I will itinerate no more. I've come through thick and thin and I do mean *thick* and thin. There have been glowing good times; and there have been desperate challenging times. I also know my congregations have often been first and my family has often been last. I've gained much along the way; but I confess that I've probably left undone more than a few things. I pray that the churches I've served know I tried to do the best I could by them. And, I pray that my family knows I love, appreciate them, and that they forgive me for times I was absent to them and unaware of their needs."

The retiree continued, "I plead with those who follow not to forget the call to participate in and contribute to the blessings of your own family life, and also not to forget to tend to your own needs for renewal. I want to leave you with this message: 'Growing comes from knowing how to face into what I call the stormy gale. But, you can't do it if you are running on "E" as in "Empty." Remember to stop and find the filling station.'"

These two stories serve as "windows" for reflecting on the lives pastors and families live. They remind us of ourselves and our stories of promise and celebration, along with stories of pain during our experiences as preachers' kids and during years in parish ministry. They remind us, too, that we all have a past story, a present story, and an unfolding story, replete with opportunities, challenges, and our choice to face into the storm wind and discover the wind or spirit of resiliency and hope. Indeed, these opening stories tell us that at points along the way, clergy family members need a place to tell about life's realities, and to receive support and inspiration sufficient for the journey forward.

But, the truth of the matter is, too frequently, the stories of clergy families become submerged or go untold because, apart from fear of complaining, life seems too busy for self-disclosure. Too frequently, the stories also become submerged or go untold because of feelings that there is either no one to hear them or no safe place in which to share openly. Moreover, there is a sense in which many clergy families struggle alone or in near silence with stories of struggle because of the perceived need to project an image of strength, or to live out a "perfect" story. These families are reticent to disclose the truth about the unique life and challenges of ministry even with other clergy families because of a conscious or unconscious fear that admitting to struggles and expressing need will block the success trajectory. But, the stories remain! They do not disappear!

What's in a Story?

In remembering our own stories and those told to us by other members of clergy families, five interrelated themes of challenge consistently appear: the challenge of **moving**, the challenge of **meeting expectations**, the challenge of **making family life count**, the challenge of **meaning-making in parsonage living**, and **managing catastrophic events** and other devastating circumstances.

Moving

Clergy families readily attest to and research affirms the issues of "the mobility syndrome" in the vocation of ordained ministry. The stories of these families are replete with experiences of grief and loss, a sense of powerlessness or loss of control, anger, fear about an unknown future and continued transience, strain on family life, and profound loneliness.[2] Of course, the issue of moving is not new,[3] but what is new for clergy (and even more for spouses and children) is an exacerbated sense of loss of viable support networks through which families experience belonging, a haven to tell stories that nurture them, and caring others to give them guidance. As one clergy spouse put it, "We're just sent adrift with little recognition that we exist or matter—and by *we*, I mean me and the children. It is true that I knew something about the lifestyle into which I married. But, being *in* it is quite a different thing."

Whether the spouses are women or men and regardless of the ages of the children, there is a cry for establishing deep and ongoing relational ties, to be valued, and to carry on consistently stable lives in communities, spousal work places, and schools. Experiencing healing responses to this cry is complicated by the market-driven culture in which we live that tends to reduce people to commodities to be bought and sold. Moreover, we live in a fast-paced technologically dominated ethos that gives people little time to engage in face-to-face interaction. Indeed, what people are internalizing is a self and materially oriented value orientation that, when mixed with high mobility, creates unbearable spheres of loneliness, lovelessness and profound anxiety.

AN INVITATION TO REFLECT

As a clergyperson, spouse, or child, recall briefly with another family member or caring other(s) your own experiences of moving. What feelings arise as you remember the experience of moving? What was good or promising about moving? What was difficult? What has helped you to deal with moving? What would be helpful in the future and how may this help be obtained?

Meeting Expectations

The book, *Recalling Our Own Stories*, highlights the tendency on the part of clergy and other caregivers to internalize and act on the myth of perfection.[4] The result of their expectations or self demands is the embrace of a perfectionistic lifestyle wherein the clergyperson feels constrained to respond to every situation and need that arises in the congregation. At the same time, the congregation and denomination place clear demands on the clergyperson. In this situation, the care of self and family is placed in the background.

Many pastors tell of the congregation and denomination "meeting syndrome" that, when combined with other pastoral responsibilities, lengthens the day and shortens the time for self and family. The timing of meetings also poses problems. While sharing our ministry stories, we recalled receiving the announcement that the annual fall minister's convocation would again be held during the weekend before the start of the new school year. This weekend was typically the final opportunity for families to bring closure to the summer break, to prepare children for their upcoming experiences in school, and for spouses who taught in the schools or were in other vocations to complete plans for the coming months. The difficulty in the announcement was that clergy were to be housed in clergy-only accommodations and, if families came, they would necessarily stay "outside the camp" at the family's expense. We recalled discussing how we would handle the situation. Our decision was that we would attend together and risk the invitation for Anne, who was not clergy, to leave. We quietly entered the meeting, remained in it together, and when asked why Anne was there, we spoke about the importance of the togetherness of families at that time and of the church's reconsideration of the meeting time.

It must be added that, associated with the perfectionistic approach to ministry is a fear of failure—of not being successful—or of not measuring up to a degree that will warrant advancement or promotion. Indeed, personal and family stress can be attributed to the individualistic, productivity, competitive values framework in which we live today and the infiltration of these values in ecclesiastical life where ministerial success models are constantly paraded before clergy before and after entering ministry.[5] As one young pastor put it, "We're called to carry out a good ministry wherever we are at a given point in time. And I intend to do just that, including in my present small church where I'm working hard to make it grow. But, it's a slow process in a place where, frankly, there is a lot of resistance. Sure, I want to progress to the big church or a significant position in the denomination. I have aspirations for advancement. I believe the same is true for other pastors. A lot depends on what happens now and along the way. I feel the pressure."

It must not be assumed that clergypersons are alone in their self-expectations and demands. Spouses and children of clergy also experience the demands of congregations for their "perfect" behavior and involvement in and beyond congregational life. In an earlier mentioned story, for example, the spouse was concerned about the church's expectation of her and how she was going to function. Both of us also recall that, even though our mothers were in vocations outside the home, they knew and complied with the congregations' expectations of them. This meant leading in the areas of women's groups, music, and church school; attending Bible study and prayer meetings; being involved in community affairs. However, the situation today differs from the past. There are increasing numbers of dual career spouses, including clergy couples with or without children, and increasing situations of husbands of women clergy whose lives move according to interests and callings external to the church with competing expectations. Moreover, there are single parent clergy families, single unmarried and divorced clergy who also respond to family needs and the expectations and demands of congregations. Conflicts, pressure, and family difficulty are consequences of persons' attempts to satisfy their calling and negotiate responses to the self's and others' expectations.

Expectations of exemplary behavior of pastors' children add to the conundrum of clergy family life. One of the experiences that surfaced in our recall of childhood in a clergy family was Ed's return home from school on a stormy day. He recalled waiting for the bus over what felt like an eternity. When the bus finally appeared, he remembered looking forward to finally getting into a dry place for a while. But, just as the bus pulled alongside, the wheels moved directly into a heightened pool of water at the curb. A big gush of slushy, murky water splashed directly into his already wet frame from his face downward. He confessed that the language he used at that point is non-repeatable even now; and it was this non-repeatable language that came forth just as the bus door opened. In full view, seated in the front seat was a staunch member of his dad's church who heard every word and frowned with appall. Ed instantly knew that, at that moment, he had failed the test of perfection and that the story of his imperfection would be shared "far and wide." Of course, his words today are, "Well, I have lived to tell it now."

The children of clergy know that they are closely watched by church members, community residents, and even by school personnel. "You know this," said a teenaged daughter of a pastor, "because somebody somewhere will say to you, 'You're Reverend _____'s daughter, aren't you?' Sometimes, they'll ask me if I'm going to be a minister too. A lot of times, I just look at them without saying anything, while I'm thinking, 'Why do they need to ask me that question?'" Another pastor's child with whom we had conversation said, "It's not so bad. My parents are pretty 'cool' about the whole thing. Although I go to church most of the time, they don't *make* me go. Their support makes all the difference." However, in another situation about which we became aware, a pastor's child had attempted suicide because of the pressures for "perfect behavior" from within the congregation and at home. What is important to add here are the findings of research that the situation of children in clergy families is not always reported by them to be negative. However, there is no question that their lifestyles are stressful, that their circumstances need to be considered, and their stories heard.[6]

The key point here is that clergy families face real challenges of meeting external and internal expectations. Deeply felt dynamics that take place within congregations complicate this reality today. The collapse of traditional family and communal networks traumatize parishioners themselves who feel the sting of purposelessness, lovelessness, and loneliness that results from our society's individualistic, competitive, materialistic, and productivity values orientation. These persons seek answers to this painful reality in congregational life. Clergy and clergy families are often expected to provide surrogate family functions that are missing in the lives of the members of the congregation. In fact, Carrie Doehring highlights the reality that clergy families are often expected to deliver perfect empathy in our current situation of network collapse. The weight of this expectation is too heavy to bear for clergy families. It becomes exceedingly burdensome, especially when the support networks for these families are minimal or non-existent.

AN INVITATION TO REFLECT

As family members, share some thoughts about what the congregation expects of you and how you feel about it. Share some thoughts about your expectations of yourselves and one another. What is most important to do when expectations of others and your own expectations collide?

Making Family Life Count

In their insightful book, *The Family: A Christian Perspective on the Contemporary Home*, Jack and Judith Balswick remind us that the family is understood as a "place where we can be naked and not ashamed (Gen. 2:25), a place where we can be who we are, free from all the demanding requirements of the outside world. Here is a place where family members can relax and be comfortable in a supportive and encouraging atmosphere. Here they do not have to hide, but can be honest and real before the others in the family."[7] This function of creating a supportive and encouraging environment where family members can be real is called transparency. In transparency, individual and family vulnerabilities do not have to be hid. The heart hungers of each family member can be exposed without fear of them being exploited or used to the family member's disadvantage. We may express our fears about ourselves and about our lack of personal adequacy and we can find courage to continue on in life, despite our human frailty and limitations.

The presence of the transparency function of the family is no less important in clergy families; and, for many of these families, carrying it out remains on the list of challenges. Without hesitation, clergy family members tell us that time is the major enemy to the kind of healthy nurturing family functioning they desire.

Clergy families want to make family life count. But, much like other families in our society today, family members often move in disparate directions, with limited collective time. Moreover, the time demand on clergypersons reduces the opportunities needed to build family rituals and maintain quality relationships. We are aware of a case, for example, in which the spouse of a clergyperson raised concern because of the daily evening church and denominational meetings and pastoral duties that the pastor felt obliged to undertake. The pastor expressed a sense of unawareness of being absent to the degree described by the spouse. As the pattern continued, the spouse decided to keep a diary for the period of one month. At the end of the month, the spouse presented the diary to the pastor and showed that, of the thirty evenings in the month, the pastor was absent twenty-eight of them. A family conference resulted not simply in the pastor's increased awareness of the problematic impact of time away from family life, but of the pastor's intentional selectivity of the kinds and numbers of meetings and duties to which response would be given.

But, in our fast-paced, techno-dominated and productivity-driven society, clergy families have become prey to the pressurized problem of immediacy into which more and more activities are "crunched" into shorter and shorter time spans, even with the abundance of so-called "time-saving devices." Recently, a seminary student reported hearing a cell-phone ring in the pulpit and observed the pastor quietly answering the phone during the choir's music ministry. Cell phones also give church members unlimited access to pastors during times at home. Yet, it is appropriate to add that clergy family members become likewise distracted by this techno-communication wizardry. Indeed, it may be fair to say that, like many others in today's world, far too many clergy families have become enslaved to time, so much so that they are yearning for freedom to rightly care for self and one another and are seeking what has become an elusive nurture and happiness in family life. The question posed by Gertrud Mueller Nelson in her book, *To Dance With God: Ritual and Community Celebration,* is an apt one to which attention must rightly be given: "Have we packed our lives with such a frantic pace in search of elusive happiness that God cannot get a word in edgewise?"[8]

The crucial concern raised above is in the word, "ritual." In order for families to function well, there needs to be time to establish and carry out family rituals. Family rituals are times spent with significant others during significant family life cycle events and transitions. The purpose of rituals is to provide family support, recognition, avenues of emotional expression of strong feelings, opportunities to strengthen relational ties, and to offer blessings for family life together. Such events require time for preparation and execution. Too often we do not create time for family meals, or celebration of family birthdays, or significant personal achievements of family members. The point is that family rituals are essential for fulfilling family life for clergy families.

In all fairness, though, we must say that there are clergy families who successfully meet the challenge of making family life count. However, they are quick to say that it takes considerable effort and forthright commitment. In one instance, a divorced clergywoman expressed her determination to be available to and intentionally connected with the lives of her children. For her, this meant placing the children as priorities, including maintaining mealtimes together, making school visits, and attending key events in the children's lives. She confessed that there have been times when competing schedules required negotiation and times when the answer in favor of her children has "turned eyebrows" and perhaps jeopardized her future ministry. But, she was clear in her view that her expectation of herself was to be both a caring, nurturing parent to her children and an example of "good enough" parenting for her congregation.

AN INVITATION TO REFLECT

Create some time as a family unit or with others to share individually with one another what is most important to you about your family. Explore what has happened in your family life that has given you joy. Then explore some aspects of your family life that you would like to see change and why. In what ways would you make changes?

Meaning-Making in Parsonage Living

Parsonage living presents many challenges to clergy families. The challenge is especially great for families in the itinerant ministry, where moving from place to place occurs. For example, many of the tensions between local congregations and clergy families are acted out in dramatic fashion around parsonage issues. Local congregations own the parsonage and consider it as a public space. This view likely attests to the continuing attribution of the parsonage as a symbol of historical close-knit village life, where doors were never locked, and neighbors could walk in unannounced. This open communal orientation presents challenges to clergy families who expect and need to achieve a sense of home and private space. In addition, parsonages in changing communities often become focal points for anxieties related to whether the church will continue to exist in its current form in the future. Congregations in these communities may expect clergy families to live in the parsonage as a sign that things will remain the same.

Overall, clergy families often describe experiences of feeling continuously under scrutiny in parsonage living. In this situation, the parsonage becomes glass house existence. From the many stories about which we are aware, it is not easy to live under the pressures of the microscopic existence that parsonage life often offers. It is possible, however, to live meaningful lives despite the pressures. An important way of discovering how that happens is through story-sharing and uncovering patterns of resilience already being used, as well as ones yet to be developed.

AN INVITATION TO REFLECT

Where and with whom have you shared the stories of your parsonage life? What parsonage stories of struggle have you held inside or are now holding inside? Where and with whom may these stories be shared, and what would you hope might happen by sharing them?

Managing Catastrophic Events and Other Devastating Circumstances

In the throes of writing this book, we were abruptly reminded of public catastrophic events experienced by clergy families. This reminder came in the wake of the massive devastation wrought by hurricanes Katrina and Rita in 2005. The gulf coast regions of Alabama, Mississippi,

Louisiana, and Texas were greatly affected by severe destruction and much attention focused on the disastrous conditions caused by wind and floods in the City of New Orleans. Many clergy families lost either their homes or churches, and some clergy families lost both. Ed was invited to work with a group of United Methodist pastors who were the survivors of both hurricanes. He heard numerous harrowing details of loss, survival, and grief not only due to destroyed homes and churches, but also because of scattered members and an uncertain future for the congregations. Likewise, he encountered remarkable stories of clergy family resilience. What emerged from this time of story-sharing was a heightened awareness of the unique impact of natural disasters on clergy families.

In addition to public catastrophic events, we are also aware that clergy families confront other devastating circumstances. Sudden and unexpected losses due to accidents, illness and death, for example, have tremendous impact on clergy families. Opportunities to tell the stories of experiences and to discover resilient practices are critical to the well being of these families.

AN INVITATION TO REFLECT

What awareness do you have of clergy families who have been affected by catastrophic loss or other devastating circumstances? What resources did they have for responding to the loss or circumstance? Describe any experience(s) of catastrophic or devastating events you have personally encountered and the ways you responded. In what ways would you say clergy families differ from other families in experiencing and responding to catastrophic events or other devastating circumstances?

The Winds of Promise and the Formation of Resilience

Our own stories and the stories of other clergy families affirm that, along the ministry journey, it is not unusual for the winds of life to bring calamity, hardship, and struggle. Indeed, the winds of life may bring us to a point where we feel ourselves to be at our wits end, much like the sailors about whom the psalmist writes in Psalm 107:23-27. In a manner similar to them, we may reel and stagger like drunkards in the midst of the waves set rolling by stormy winds prompted by the command of God. And, like the sailors, we cry out to God in our trouble (Psalm, 107:28), not fully knowing what the response might be. Or, like the disciples in the Markan story, who encountered a terrifying windstorm while passing by boat from one place to another, we cry out in fear of dying in the presence of a sleeping Jesus (Mark 4:35-39).

Yet, we discover often to our surprise that our resilience in the form of simply waiting on God and being of good courage results in our recognition that God has not abandoned us. Or, we realize that even as our wisdom appears to fail in our attempt to discern the way forward, resilience emerges in our anticipation of God's generating or hope-building presence, guidance, and perception of God's dong a new thing (Isaiah 43:18-21). Our expectation of this eschatological activity of God opens us to an experience of the winds of promise that is akin to the psalmist's testimony of God's coming "upon the wings of the wind" in the throes of distress (Psalm 18:10). The point here is that resilience does not negate our confession that we are at our "wits end," or that all we know to be wise has diminished or has been "swallowed up" to use the words of commentator J. Clinton McCann, Jr.[9] We may find ourselves voicing the pregnant question of the disciples in the Markan story: "Teacher, do you not care that we are perishing" (Mark 4:38b). But, resilience comes in the midst of calamity when we dare to anticipate God's response.[10]

The kind of resilience to which we are referring is a spiritual elasticity that is also borne of resilient faith in God's living and purpose-revealing presence. This kind of faith claims along the way, as Job did in the midst of mayhem, "I know that my Redeemer lives." And, this faith affirms that the message of divine purpose given by God to Judean exiles in Babylon recorded in the book of Jeremiah can be applied to the unique circumstances of clergy families today: "For I know the plans I have for you, says the Lord; plans for your welfare and not for harm, to give you a future with hope" (Jeremiah 29:11). Resilience is built by our claim that God not only has a plan and purpose for our unfolding story, but God also reveals the plotline on which we can count. God's plan and purpose are innermost aspects of the winds of promise. Resilience comes in God's revealing God's plotline in ways that give direction in the throes of current circumstances and lead toward God's ends and purposes. Resilience blossoms by our embrace of these aspects and by our dependence upon

God, not as an emergency measure, but as a way of life.[11] In fact, this kind of resilient faith counters the prevailing view in current day society of self-sufficiency. Such a faith says that we cannot make it by ourselves.

What we are saying here is that resilience is borne of our reaching out to God, who invites our outreach and cries for help in the messiness of life, and we anticipate God's response—God's *ruach* or breath or "wind" to give us renewed life and sustenance along the way. Moreover, resilient faith opens the way for our wanting to tell our stories and finding or building environments within which the stories of family members can be shared in the presence of caring others. Resilient faith also allows for God's vitalizing and sustaining Spirit to be felt in mutual sharing and caring. In this sense, we recognize that God's wind of promise becomes present and active through others with whom we entrust our stories. And, God's wind of promise becomes active through our listening and caring for others. Through shared story, we recognize the veracity of Joan Chittister's profound statement that, "struggle changes us; it grows us up. It takes the dew off the rose and the gilt off the silver. It turns the fantasies of life into reality. But it does more than that. It also gives life depth and vision, insight and understanding, compassion and character. It not only transforms us, it makes us transforming as well."[12] We recognize God's sustaining grace in the form of needed wisdom and the discovery of existing capacities with which to move forward on life's journey.

The Necessity of Engaging a Story-Sharing Process

Moving forward requires clergy families to give voice to the real stories of everyday life. It requires persons' daring to tell the stories of challenge in a caring environment and an audacious anticipation of God's hope-building, purpose-revealing, and sustaining presence and guidance, as well as their discovery of personal capacities and needed actions. On this basis, we invite clergy family members to explore patterns of resilience already being used in the face of the challenges of moving, meeting expectations, making family life count, meaning-making amidst glass-house living, and managing catastrophic events. Clergy families often experience these challenges as oppressive and even as terrorizing. This is especially the case given congregations' oft-times expectation of clergy families to be present and perfect in order that parishioners have anchors in the throes of life's uncertainties, and other church or denominational givens. In a sense, the challenges may be viewed as non-negotiable or as unchanging parts of clergy family existence. In this light, the task is not to find ways of overthrowing these realities. Rather, it is important to discover how clergy family members have found and may yet meet the challenges in helpful, hope-filled, and wholeness affirming ways.

As a clergy couple, we have discovered that the key to finding out how clergy families become resilient in the face of these gigantic challenges is found in the stories these families tell and retell. Many hidden resources surface only when we tell and retell the stories of our lives. As clergy family stories unfold, plotlines pushing and pulling the family into significance and meaning can be discerned. These plotlines can be drawn on and built upon in order to nurture the family as it seeks to carry out its many family tasks and as ordained or official clergyperson(s) carry out his or her tasks of ministry.

Plotlines give direction, meaning, and purpose for those called into ministry. These plotlines begin as clergy members become cognizant of their original awareness that a form of ministry will be their life work. These plotlines continue to develop in cases where the clergy are married and where children are involved. The task of married clergy is to come to grips with what it means to be a clergy family. Moreover, the task involves finding ways to build a couple and family story that reflects the reality that spouses will be conscripted or drafted into the ministry along with any children they may have. At each stage of the family process—mating and formation leading from dating to engagement and marriage, expansion by having children, contraction when children grow up and leave, and retirement from the ministry—the family must build a nurturing story that includes their formation of resilience in facing challenges confronting them. This construction of a nurturing story remains even though the impact of the challenges on clergy family members may differ for clergy couples, single pastors, and for divorced or remarried clergy, as well as for female versus male clergy-headed families.

It is only when clergy families tell and retell their stories as they confront the unique challenges of their lives that they discover resilient plotlines. This awareness is the major thrust of the story-sharing process presented here. There are no magic remedies or strategies to be presented. Resilient stories emerge only when clergy families engage in intentional story-sharing.

We remember our first years in the parish ministry in the late 1960s. We lived in a small town in Massachusetts when Ed was a middler in seminary. Not long after our arrival, the director of the Massachusetts Council of Churches came and began a discussion about cooperation in ministry with the five churches in this small town. Many things came out of this discussion, but the most meaningful to us as a young couple was the discovery of four clergy families. Together, we began meeting regularly to share stories and experiences. We became a support group within which we explored what it meant to face the demands and expectations of being ministers and ministers' families in a small town in Massachusetts. We were the only African Americans in town, but we learned invaluable lessons about sharing and handling the necessities of couples and families in ministry. Through the process of sharing our stories, we struggled and grew as clergy families.

Following two years in this small town, we moved to an urban area in middle Massachusetts where we spent the next six years. We formed clergy family groupings that met regularly for a variety of reasons. These groups were either all African American, or were integrated depending on the function or on a denominational or ecumenical basis. During this period of being a clergy family, we took for granted that meeting as clergy families was essential for our survival in ministry. We learned that such meetings and opportunities for clergy families is not a luxury; it is essential. Moreover, we developed a keen awareness that we need Sabbath time and retreat times to tell and share our stories as we seek to discover the plotlines that enable us to be resilient despite the demands of ministry.

Over years of additional opportunities to share our own stories with clergy families and lead clergy family story-sharing, we have also discovered that in story-sharing, plotlines and the winds of promise are linked. We are convinced that the wisdom of God is encountered daily as the story of God unfolds and shapes our lives. The plotline is a dynamic force pushing and pulling us toward God's future. As indicated earlier, the wind is a fitting metaphor that characterizes how plotlines work. God's unfolding plotline is like the wind that blows, catches us up, and takes us in the desired direction of meaning and wholeness. Being caught up in God's plotline is the source of resiliency. Story-sharing enables this discovery or re-discovery.

How the Book Unfolds

In the following chapters, we invite clergy families to enter into some intentional times of story-sharing—times of family "Sabbath." Our invitation is for clergy family members in individual, family unit, or group settings with or without a guide to engage in story-sharing in order to discover or rediscover the source of the winds of promise and the resilience that resides in them in the unique journey of life in congregations. Specifically, we invite clergy family members into a process of story-sharing directed toward catharsis, relating empathically, and moving forward through reflection, discovery and discernment of God's presence and the self's resilience. Entitled "Facing Forward: Engaging and Building Practices of Resilience," chapter one will describe the story-sharing process in detail.

In chapters two through five, we will guide families through the process described in chapter one. In each of the chapters, we will share our own personal stories, as well as additional clergy family vignettes, as means of inviting your story-sharing around the four challenges presented here in the prologue. In particular, chapter two will focus on the challenge of moving. The chapter invites story-sharing around the tremendous stress moving exerts on family resources.

Chapter three will invite story-sharing around the challenge of meeting expectations. This chapter gives attention to the traditional expectations congregations have of clergy families and how these expectations can be intimidating. The chapter also invites an exploration of how these expectations may be handled.

The challenge of making family life count will be the emphasis in chapter four. Here, the story-sharing process will challenge you to openly reflect on your understanding and experiences of family life and the extent to which you make family life count. The chapter also invites you to consider family rituals and activities that make a family resilient, transparent, real, and supportive.

Chapter five will center on meaning-making in parsonage living. Specific attention focuses on story-sharing about challenges emerging in parsonage living, resilient practices that help families confront the challenges, and ways to form a meaningful sense of home amidst glasshouse living.

In chapter six we explore insights gleaned from working with a number of clergy families who were survivors of hurricanes Katrina and Rita, as well as families who face other kinds of sudden and unexpected losses. We have entitled this chapter "Managing Catastrophic Events and Other Devastating Circumstances."

An epilogue entitled "The Journey Forward: A Matter of Time" concludes the book, and focuses on the need to re-conceptualize time and create or re-create steps needed to ensure a promising relational journey for clergy families.

CHAPTER ONE

Facing Forward: Story-Sharing and Building Practices of Resilience

But one thing I do, forgetting what lies behind and straining forward
to what lies ahead, I press on toward the goal for the prize
of the upward call of God in Christ Jesus.

—PHILIPPIANS 3:13B

A summer journey through the Colorado Rockies became a spontaneous detour from the route originally planned by Anne's parents. Even though the alternate route lengthened the return trip home, it was preferred not simply because of the scenic grandeur, but because it added time to the first family vacation in many years of parish life.

After traveling a considerable distance in mountainous terrain bathed in sunlight, the sky became gradually transformed into darkened billowing clouds. Then, the wind came and a mixture of hail and rain, lightning and thunder followed. At a particular high point on a curve of the two-lane highway the car, with Anne's dad at the wheel, began to skid toward the edge of a cliff. There was no guardrail to slow or stop what looked like impending disaster. Anne's grandmother yelled from the back seat, and the children joined in, "Turn around! Turn back!" In that critical moment, Dad somehow returned the car to the road's center and replied "We can't turn back! There's only one way to go, and that's forward."

It is important that we share this story here because it symbolizes in a profound way our lives growing up in clergy families and our own adult lives as clergy and spouse. The journey for us has unfolded in ways not too dissimilar from the experience in the Colorado Rockies. Like other clergy families with whom we have had the privilege of sharing stories, there have been planned (and unplanned) detours, seasons of delight and storms, fear of the unexpected, and discovery of a way out of no way. In the midst of it all, there has been the lesson to learn and relearn especially in challenging times: "We can't—indeed we won't—turn back! There's only one way to go, and that's forward!"

Of course, the question is: "How do we move forward?" In the prologue, we suggested that moving forward has to do with our discovering or re-discovering the promising wind of God's grace—God's Spirit or *ruach*—along the way. Moving forward means seeing and embracing a sense of purpose and hope that is built on our knowing God's for-us-ness as the driving force—the wind beneath our unfolding story plot. Don Friesen describes the wind of hope as the wind of God's Spirit that allows us to soar, for it inspires the kind of aspiration to press on toward the goal of the heavenly call of God about which the Apostle Paul speaks in his letter to the Philippians (Philippians 3:12-14).[1] Friesen's reference is to a kind of purposive hope that emerges even in seemingly hopeless circumstances and is not deterred by the toughness of life or by setbacks.[2] This stance is, in fact, a pivotal form of resilient faith.

There are related practices of resilience that carry clergy families along the forward journey. Resilient practices are strategic activities clergy family members perform. These activities help clergy families confront forthrightly the realities of periodic moving to unfamiliar surroundings, meeting non-negotiable expectations, making family life count while living in a parsonage and the public arena, and managing catastrophic events. Invariably, the nature of these practices emerges in story-sharing. Specifically, in telling especially the stories of challenge, clergy family members recall details of how they were able to continue on the journey through specific actions or positive changes prompted by their own decisions. Sometimes, the presence of resilience emerging in story-sharing is surprising to the story-teller, thereby prompting the story-teller to say, "At the time, I wasn't aware that what I was doing or how our family handled the situation was helpful. I can see now that we really did some things well." This kind of recognition of existing resilient practices emerging through story-sharing opens the way for clergy families to claim and build on the tenacity and strength that is within them, as well as to explore new or additional practices. Importantly, exploring new resilient practices in the process of story-sharing serves as an enabling tool for clergy families' creation of approaches to living out the unfolding story in positive ways.

We want to emphasize here that story-sharing is pivotal to the discovery and ongoing formation of resilient faith through which clergy families discover an unfolding story plot through a vital relationship with God. Moreover, story-sharing is vital to clergy families' discovery and exploration of resilient practices. For some, story-sharing may not come easily. It will mean shedding inhibitions or fears of self-disclosure. For others, it will mean creating a time—enough time—for stories to unfold. For all who embark upon the experience of shared story, it will mean making sense of the stories and envisioning not only what facing forward means, but also what must be done to move forward with purpose and hope.

Our purpose in this chapter is to provide a preparatory framework for story-sharing that offers opportunity for discovering or re-discovering resilient faith and for engaging and building practices of resilience in the face of the challenges of clergy family life. The story-sharing framework includes the following five primary practices:

- The practice of unmasking;
- The practice of inviting catharsis;
- The practice of relating empathically;
- The practice of unpacking the story; and
- The practice of discerning and deciding the way forward.

In what follows, we will describe each of these practices.

The Practice of Unmasking

We have already mentioned in the prologue that moving, meeting expectations, making family life count, meaning-making amidst glass house living, and managing catastrophic events are powerful, personally-lived stories of clergy families. But, the full nature and depth of these stories may remain submerged or stilled within family members, while at the same time, there is a deep yearning to give the personal account of what has happened or is happening. For this reason, unmasking is the first practice in the process of story-sharing.

The Nature of Unmasking

Telling our stories is an event of unmasking the self and the self's life experiences as clergy family members. Unmasking refers to our allowing internal and unspoken happenings and circumstances of our lives—challenges and promise—to come to life in narrative form. Thus, we may also refer to sharing our stories as "narrative unmasking." In sharing, we give voice to the hidden dimensions of our life realities in the presence of the listener(s). And, we become listeners to the concrete realities of others. Importantly, telling our stories also opens the way for the self's hearing in a manner not possible when stories remain unspoken or held within us. Sharing paves the way for seeing, feeling, and thinking openly in the presence of and with the help of others. Indeed, it is difficult to think through clearly what we do not say aloud. In our silence, we risk becoming objects of our own stories, rather than subjects of these stories with the capacity to voice them, to think and feel deeply about them, and to envision new ways of acting on them. We are not just passive actors in story-telling and listening. Rather, in story-sharing, we become creative agents in seeing and assessing our lives and in envisioning God's activity and plan for our lives. In the process of sharing our stories, we see ourselves and others beyond the masks that our faces portray.

Our use of story-sharing as an expression of unmasking in the relational context of clergy families builds on the storied process we have used in marriage enrichment retreats. What we learned about our own and others' un-masking in these retreats has become an important guide for similar unmasking in clergy families. Specifically, we have led a variety of retreats for over twenty years. We began first with marriage enrichment retreats for clergy and non-clergy couples that focused on the expressed needs of couples to develop deepening meaning and satisfaction in their marriages, given the fragile nature of marriage in our contemporary society. We discovered that persons were desirous and hopeful of improving their relationships, and that they desperately needed a place and space where they could tell their stories.

To our surprise, we found that couples utilized the time to tell their stories with excitement and enthusiasm. Many wondered why they had not discovered the method of telling and retelling stories of their relationships much earlier. In fact, many re-discovered that story-sharing about their past relationships with significant others characterized their courtship journeys prior to marriage. Moreover, they rediscovered how important this sharing of their stories during courtship was to the initial glue that cemented their relationship and their intent to become marriage partners. Yet, as their lives unfolded after marriage, they forgot the important lessons related to sharing their stories together. Thus, at the marriage retreats they began to experience a sense of renewal in the marital relationships based on their story-sharing. They rediscovered what they had already known but had forgotten. Consequently, our first model of marriage enrichment engaged couples in retelling their courtship and engagement stories. We had them recall the time when they met, what they saw in each other, and what they appreciated about each other. Eventually, the reasons why they married in the first place began to surface, and this form of recollecting became the basis of their renewing their marital relationship.

In those early days of marital enrichment workshops, we relied on the work of Howard Clinebell entitled *Intimate Marriage.*[3] The model was called the IMM or "the intimate marriage method." What was significant about this method was that it began with helping couples begin marital enrichment by recalling the less conflicting stories of their married lives and relationships, and then moving toward the more conflicting dimensions once the nurturing aspects of their relationships were solidly rediscovered.

We also utilized the method of story-sharing of David and Vera Mace that we encountered in the early 1980s while attending one of their workshop demonstrations. They shared their own stories of marital life as a model for couples to follow as the couples shared their own stories. Once we told our marital stories related to a specific topic or concern, we invited couples to share their own stories together in the time and place provided by the retreat.

We discovered that our own unmasking through sharing stories of our relationship re-enforced our marital relationship. Not only this, but our retelling our own stories and others' story-sharing also did several key things that we realized as essential for any vital marital and family relationship. First, in telling our relationship stories, we discovered that an overarching narrative story emerged, characterized by convictions and beliefs about why we met, why we cared for each other, when we married, and why we were put together by a divine design for the purpose of ministry. Consequently, we discovered that the process of telling our own stories was not a mere perfunctory exercise. Rather, it was a life saving resource for reminding us of our purposes for being together as a marital couple in the eyes of God. In short, we discovered that our marital story was connected to God's unfolding story of salvation, and that it was not just human attraction that put us together. We discovered that God was calling us together for the purpose of ministry.

Second, story-sharing revealed the values that we cherished in our relationship. The values are commitment to fidelity, the significance of constantly connecting to each other's heart hungers, the importance of emotional and sexual intimacy, the ongoing need to clarify our relationships with others, and our common personal and couple calling to be disciples of Jesus Christ. We found things we liked and disliked about the family into which we were born, and we also discovered personal traits that we either needed to let go, or hold onto in ways that improved our lives.

Third, we gradually discovered how God was intimately involved in our personal and our marital lives. Eventually, a master narrative emerged that continually let us know what our purpose was and is as a married couple. Consequently, our whole marital life in the parish and in theological education has been to nurture the growth of persons, as well as to help people improve their marital relationships.

As our story has revealed, both of us have used the power of sharing stories as an unmasking experience through which the nurture of growth and improvement in relationships could occur. Similarly, this understanding of narrative applies to clergy families, regardless of the family makeup and congregational setting. Story-sharing is an essential dimension in life that allows us to tell and hear the realities of our lives often held in silence. This is what we call narrative unmasking. This sort of letting out the inner story is pivotal to orienting our lives together as individuals, marital partners, and families in meaningful ways. Moreover, revealing the self and the self's experiences as clergy family members through narrative unmasking opens the way for us to see God at work in our lives. It enables us to link our individual, marital, and family stories with God's unfolding and promising story of liberation, salvation, and redemption. Finally, we view narrative unmasking as a vital way of renewing our lives and updating the purpose for which God called us as individuals, marital partners, and family members. This is what we call the unmasking of a master story.

Guides to Unmasking

Each member of the clergy family experiences clergy family life in his or her own particular way. And, each family member sees and responds to what happens to him or her from the perspective of beliefs and convictions he or she holds about being in a clergy family. Likewise, family members typically share certain beliefs and convictions. These shared views inform what family members say and do in family life together and how the family unit and individual members interact among themselves and the world beyond them.

The beliefs and convictions of clergy family members form a mythology that cannot be ignored in the story-telling process. Indeed, the mythology may be a key factor in developing individual and family resilience in the face of challenges. For example, one key factor in long lasting marriages is having a common story or narrative that sustains the marriage through difficult times. Consequently, an important entry point to telling our stories of moving, meeting expectations, making family life count, meaning-making, and managing catastrophic events is the exploration of clergy family mythology. As family members, consider three key areas of family ministry mythology and questions within each area.

- Awareness of the Uniqueness of Clergy Family Membership
  1. When did you first realize that being a clergy family was different from other families?
  2. Describe the circumstances, people, and concerns that brought this awareness to your attention?
  3. How did you feel about this realization?
  4. What were some of the immediate consequences of your original awareness?
  5. What significance or meanings would you assign to the consequences?
  6. Can you assign a name, story, or characterization of your beliefs and convictions about being a clergy family?

- Influence of Clergy Family Membership Over Time
  1. Is it possible to talk about how your awareness of being a clergy family member has influenced your thoughts, beliefs, and behavior over time? If so, describe your unfolding view of being a clergy family member. If not, say something about why it is not possible at this time to talk about your unfolding view.
  2. What name(s) would you assign to influences on your thoughts, beliefs and behavior in your unfolding journey as a clergy family member?

3. What has helped you respond to problems or challenges that you as a clergy family member have confronted?
4. How may you summarize ways in which your original awareness of being a clergy family has changed over time?
5. What are the positive consequences of your beliefs and convictions about being a clergy family member? What are ways in which your beliefs and convictions have contributed to your resilience to external challenges?
6. What would you say are the negative consequences of your beliefs and convictions?

- Cultural Influences on Views of Clergy Family Life
  1. What cultural views and values help shape your convictions and beliefs about being a clergy family?
  2. What cultural views and values help you develop patterns of resilience in the face of challenge?

A Guide to Telling the Story

The specific structure or order in which we tell our stories will often vary from person to person and according to the particular story being told. For example, after answering the key questions in the preceding section, participants in a group of clergy families were invited to tell their stories of a catastrophic event that all of them had experienced. One person began at the point of the impact of the event on the clergy family, and then moved backward prior to the event itself, followed by a movement forward through the event once again to the present time. In another instance, the story-telling began with the details of the catastrophic event followed by its aftermath and impact on the family. However, we have learned through other experiences of clergy family story-telling that it is not unusual for persons to say, "I don't know where to begin. There is so much to tell. Where do I begin?" Particularly in these instances, it is helpful to be given a story structure, such as the following:[4]

1. Describe the scene or setting of the story. Where and when did the issue or concern about moving, meeting expectations, and others take place?
2. Introduce the problem. What was the nature of this issue or con-

cern related to moving meeting expectations, and etc.?
3. Tell who is involved. Who were the major actors in the scene?
4. Describe the tensions that exist.
5. Reveal the unfolding plot or plotline if it can be discerned.
6. Highlight the climax of the story or the resolution.

We are aware of persons for whom the unmasking process or ease of sharing openly is quite difficult, even though the need to tell their stories is quite deep. We recall one instance in which a story of pain in moving was so painful that the only mode of telling it was to recite the words of the song, "Sometimes I feel Like a Motherless Child, a Long Way From Home."[5] This instance suggests that songs, symbols, poems, and art may provide the opening needed for some persons to tell their stories.

There are other outcomes of telling stories beyond their uses as expressions of the unmasking of the self and the selves experiences. We now turn to the importance of catharsis.

The Practice of Inviting Catharsis

As part of sharing stories of our lives as clergy family members, it is important to create a safe space within which persons can experience catharsis. Cathartic moments are occasions when we feel freed to unburden ourselves by "telling it like it is." In these moments, we may freely sigh, moan, cry, laugh, or express the feelings that arise in the throes of our story-sharing. In these cathartic moments, we express that which requires not simply release, but attention.

Whereas unmasking allows the hiddenness of our stories to come to light, catharsis is the "unburdening" of the heaviness that has accompanied holding onto a troubling or challenging experience or circumstance. In catharsis, we arrive at a point where we say, "Finally I have said what's on my heart," or "Blessed relief! It's out now." The importance of moments of catharsis was highlighted in the memory of a clergy family member who had participated in a small group experience of story-telling. The words after reviewing the occasion of the group sharing were: "Today I still cry when I remember how incredible it felt to be given a full hour to talk about our life and our transition without interruption among others who had recently faced similar experiences."

Relating Empathically

A part of the reminiscence of the clergy family member who spoke of the importance of catharsis had to do with the empathic connectedness resulting from group story-telling and story-listening. This kind of relating with others was captured in the words: "It was equally powerful to be trusted with the stories of others. It was truly a holy moment." On a different occasion, a clergy spouse responded to another spouse's story of struggle: "In your story, I have heard my own. I need to say to you: 'I understand.'"

Invariably, when we enter into sharing significant moments, events, struggles, tragedies, accomplishments, and celebrations of our lives, we discover the nearness we are to others and others to us. Indeed, whether in a family unit or group setting, our telling and listening allow us to step into another's realm of being. Our empathic connectedness builds as we listen attentively to one another's stories and receive stories and the story-tellers as gifts. As gifts, we discover parts of another's life that is akin to ours, as well as the uniqueness of our experiences and how we have traveled life's journey as clergy family members.

In story-telling and story-listening, we affirm the realness of one another's journey, the significance of remembering, and the need not simply to share our stories. We need to make sense of them. Importantly, our focus moves beyond the self's story and turns to the others. Empathic connectedness means that we feel with and for one another; whereupon, mutual support builds and the discovery of insights, resilience, and a way forward begins to emerge. We become to one another the caring, nurturing presence of Christ. Empathic connectedness becomes an experience of holiness. This holy experience of God with us through the mutual support of those around us, and the same given to others by us, serves as a pathway for our movement toward the winds of promise. The mutual support that emerges from empathic connectedness also creates the ground for the tough work of unpacking our stories.

Unpacking Our Stories

We have found that the master story needs to be updated periodically in our lives because internal changes take place in families and new challenges occur that are external to the family. We have identified several basic challenges that we describe as moving, meeting expectations, making family life work, and meaning-making. We have also added a special category called managing catastrophic events.

The updating dimension of our stories draws on methods that can be called spiritual renewal exercises, re-authoring, and editing. Key here is the idea that we need to periodically revisit the overarching stories that inform our lives as clergy families, which are implicit or explicit. This revisiting needs to take place at those critical times when we are facing transitions in our lives. In order to engage the process of revisiting the overarching story under-girding our lives, we have been utilizing a helpful metaphor of family ministry mythology.

We call the family ministry story that informs what ministers do and how they relate to others a mythology.[6] A mythology is neither fiction nor an untruth. Rather, it is a shared story constructed and created by clergy families that informs what they do with each other as well as what they do in relationship to those outside their immediate family, especially to those who are in the church. The family ministry mythology includes the actual beliefs and convictions family members hold about being members where one or more family members are ordained in the Christian ministry. Such beliefs and convictions are individual as well as shared by family members. These beliefs are convictions, are dynamic in nature, and they can be updated, downgraded, revised, and abandoned. As these beliefs and convictions change over time, the behavior and relationships within the family and between others also change.

The significance of the family ministry mythology is that it is the key factor in the development of family resilience when clergy families confront the concerns and issues this book is addressing. Everything that clergy families encounter is filtered through this constructed mythology, and this myth helps the family interpret and respond to what it is confronting. For example, the family ministry mythology is often a nurturing influence when the family is in crisis, and it functions as a shared story that gives perspective and meaning to them in difficult times.

An example of the function of a family ministry mythology is the expression "this too shall pass." This is an awareness that obstacles and difficulties that confront us are not lasting. They run a specific course, and the job of the family is to stay the course until the time of challenge is over, and things can return to a period of normalcy.

We are not assuming that the family ministry mythology is explicit. Our assumption is that it exists in some form, and it is functional and active within all clergy families. Moreover, we assume that awareness of the family mythology by clergy family members is a plus and will increase its resilience when clergy family members confront problems. Greater awareness of the beliefs and convictions that they have will enable each family member to grow and thrive when the family is in crisis. It is important for the family myth to facilitate family growth and provide support and nurture for each family member. Therefore, the first task in unpacking our stories is to become aware of our implicit beliefs and convictions informing how we behave and relate to others as clergy families.

There are certain key questions that must be asked as a means to help clergy family members become aware of their beliefs and convictions about their functioning as clergy families. A series of questions can be asked that will help family members give voice to the myth. The first question is: When did you realize that being a member of a clergy family was different from those in other families? In our own situation as "preacher's kids," parishioners reminded us that we were to be model children who were to be leaders for other children. This was a daily occurrence even at school.

Following the exploration of the first awareness of being a clergy family member, another level of exploration relates to exploring the consequences of this awareness on our lives. The major concern is how the awareness affected our adolescent and adult selves related to feelings of worth and being different. Moreover, how do you feel today when you recall this original awareness? Reliving the feelings today may bring some sadness; yet, we realize that such experiences become essential contributors of who we are in positive and creative ways. Importantly, what comes to mind need not be entirely negative. Our lives as clergy and in clergy families are filled not simply with moments of challenge, but with occasions of joy, grace, humor, and accomplishment that are remembered with gratitude.

After recollecting our original awareness of being a member of a clergy family and comparing it with where we are today, in the next phase we give a name to what we recalled. In giving a name, we capture in a word or image the beliefs and convictions that make up our views of being a member of a clergy family. For example, one young adult growing up in a clergy family said that it was a "bummer." Another young adult named her experience growing up in a clergy family as "blessed," because her clergy mother would always allow her to share her feelings about what it was like being a preacher's kid. Moreover, she felt her mother supported her when she did not want to be bothered with the church people. She said, "My mother wanted me to grow up and not be intimidated by the expectations of others." Others describe the experiences of being in a clergy family as a "glass house where everyone is looking in on you." In short, the purpose of naming is to capture in a metaphor or image the nature of the family ministry myth so that it is possible to assess the influence it has on family members over time.

Clergy family members assessing the impact of the family ministry myth on family members is very important. For example, the negative as well as the positive aspects of the family ministry myth can be identified. Moreover, the plotline and resilient factors can be identified. Ultimately, the issue is for each family member to assess the impact on him or her and whether the myth is growth inhibiting or growth enhancing. In our cases aspects of our family ministry mythology have been healthy and other aspects have been unhealthy. We have built on the healthy aspects, and we have tried to revise or edit the negative aspects through personal and marital therapy, and a variety of renewal experiences.

Finally, each person needs to put his or her family myth into historical perspective. For example, there are contrasting expectations for how clergy family members should handle the expectations placed on family members. Some expectations include keeping family imperfections hidden in order to keep up appearances. Another expectation is for family members to be transparent and allow parishioners to learn and grow from family difficulties. For example, the concept of the pastor and pastor's families as wounded healers, made popular by Henry Nouwen, has characterized contemporary expectations for ministers and their families in certain religious traditions. In the 1970s and 80s Brooks Holifield urged clergy and their families not to conform to or try to escape the expectations of clergy and clergy families.[7] He felt that pastors particularly needed to help parishioners explore their expectations of ministers. In other words, he felt ministers needed to learn to not be intimidated by expectations of parishioners so they could help the parishioners develop more healthy expectations.

Hollifield presents two contemporary myths clergy families can develop that have historical and contemporary significance. The first is the image of the clergyperson as a gentile person. The gentile pastor is one who is industrious, enterprising, cultured and refined. This person must put on a public persona or mask and always portray an image of complete respectability. The goal is to keep up one's image and reputation. The second historical image is that of the warm and caring pastor who was an ordinary human being, who was transparent and shared mutual relationships of warmth with others. These images reflect different periods of history. It is important to use the gentile model or the transparent model to access the nature of the clergy family mythology.

As already indicated, the purpose of assessing the family ministry myth is to discern whether it is a resource for family resilience. The critical question is whether or not the clergy family mythology will enable family members to move forward in the future.

Moving Forward

As indicated, the processes involved in identifying and updating the family ministry mythology are for the purposes of finding resources for family resilience as the family moves forward in the congregational setting and ministry. However, such resources are simply found within the clergy family mythology. The resources and reservoir of resilience are also found in the master story or faith story that lies beneath all of our clergy family myths. The master faith story underlying all of our family myths is the unfolding story of God helping us to renew, upgrade, edit, or re-author our clergy family myths so that it becomes a resilient resource supporting our ability as a family to carrying out the tasks of being a clergy family. Consequently, telling our own stories as clergy family members enables us to identify the plotline behind our stories. Moreover, we can assess whether or not the plotline is consistent with God's unfolding plot to liberate and redeem the world.

The way forward is for clergy family members to identify the images, symbols and metaphors that surface during the assessment phases of the clergy family mythology. These symbols provide clues to the nature of the plotline behind the mythology. For example, some of the images that surfaced when working with those clergy families who were survivors of Hurricane Katrina and Rita were hospitality, host, pilgrim, exile, strangers in a foreign land, and many others. These images had roots in the Old and New Testaments, and they revealed connections to God's unfolding story of salvation in the midst of very difficult circumstances. Thus, the way forward is to find the links between the clergy family's myth and the master story of God's unfolding work in our midst. The point is that the way forward only makes sense when visualized in light of God's unfolding plan and story of salvation.

The ultimate key to resilience is the linking of our story with God's unfolding story. Linking is not only our own efforts. God seeks to draw us into God's story so that our lives and stories are more fulfilling. There is no way for our clergy family mythologies to be adequate enough to handle what we confront in ministry. They are only made adequate through the unfolding plot of God. Our resilience, then, comes from God behind our stories, rather than from our stories.

As preacher's kids, we have access to the story behind our clergy family myths. Children have personal myths that are being formed and shaped as they participate in clergy families, as well as in the life of congregations. Eventually, the myths they are forming also become resilient sources of strength. Thus, the way forward needs to include ways that parents and local churches can help their children build strong personal myths that are resources of strength and identity.

> Our major thesis is that the conditions clergy families confront in contemporary life in congregations are given and will not easily change. Moreover, tenacity and strength to move forward relies heavily on mature and healthy clergy family myths.

Applying the Practices

The practices of unmasking, inviting catharsis, relating empathically, unpacking the story and discerning and deciding movement forward which we have proposed in this chapter are central to clergy family story-sharing. Whether in story-sharing around moving, meeting expectations, making family life count, meaning-making amidst glass-house living, and managing catastrophic events, we find these five practices to be invaluable means of getting in touch with purpose and hope for the unfolding journey. We end this chapter with the following visual representation of the linkage between the story-sharing practices focused on clergy family resilience and clergy family challenges.

A Format for Applying Practices to Challenges

	Practice of Unmasking	Practice of Inviting Catharsis	Practice of Relating Empathically	Practices of Unpacking the Story	Practice of Moving Forward
Challenge of Moving					
Challenge of Meeting Expectations					
Challenge of Making Family Life Count					
Challenge of Meaning-Making					
Challenge of Managing Catastrophic Events					

CHAPTER TWO

Meeting Expectations

"Responsibility is . . . about understanding how much of what needs to be done or what we would like to see done can be in our own hands."[1]

Ever-present and high expectations are a powerfully felt part of the lives of clergy families. As members of these families, we become fully aware, sometimes quite painfully, from congregations and the public beyond them of the roles we are to assume, the kinds and qualities of behaviors to be demonstrated, and the values we are to uphold. Through their expectations, congregations—and the public—reveal and affirm the public character of being clergy and clergy families.[2] In the publication, *Educating Clergy: Teaching Practices and Pastoral Imagination*, Charles Foster and his colleagues say that "the clergy may be among the most public of professions."[3] The clergy family does not escape this reality.

Clergy family members also bring to congregational life our own sets of expectations, including what we imagine for ourselves, for one another, and for the congregation. These expectations derive from our values framework, our age or stage, our cultural and family background, or other mediating factors. In varying degrees, what we highlight as important to the character and quality of the lives we live in and beyond congregational life may be consistent with the congregation's views. Or, we may discover widely conflicting expectations.

The question is: "How is it possible for clergy families to move ahead, especially amidst publicly expressed and conflicting expectations?" It is clear from our own stories and the stories clergy family members have shared with us that specific practices of resilience are not simply needed but must be identified and affirmed in order to assist family members' dealing with expectations. In this chapter, we invite your engagement in the story-sharing process outlined in chapter one as means of uncovering these practices. In order to begin the process, we will recall scenes that focus on expectations in our own personal journeys in clergy families, as well as several brief vignettes of other clergy families. A guide to story-sharing and reflection around the issue of expectations and the presence and formation of practices of resilience will follow these stories.

Our Stories

During our years as children in minister's families, both of us knew well the image our siblings, our mothers, and we were expected to portray in various congregations along the way. Likewise, these images persisted in our own ministry journey. What follows are particular scenes of our stories.

Anne's Story

There was no mistaking the mantel of leadership or participation in music and Sunday school often placed on me, as well as the same–plus "women's work"–given to my mother. My siblings were likewise expected to be present and active in age-level programs. Importantly, there seemed to be an invisible attendance record that monitored our fulfillment of the congregation's expectation of consistent attendance for all of us at Sunday worship and other church-sponsored events.

Satisfying the expectations appeared to be inescapable, because the congregations and my dad who was the ordained clergy in the family articulated clearly the view that my siblings, our mother, and I were needed as clergy family members. In candor, these responsibilities were not spurned. They became pathways for positive affirmation and identity formation. I honed my gifts in music and teaching in these roles; and congregations affirmed and applauded these gifts. Yet, honestly, while I welcomed the appreciation I reckoned as love resulting from my compliant behavior, the absence of choice in early adolescence created a particular sense of sadness and a hindrance to my fullest exercise of independent thinking and acting. The choices of others to do or not to do what they wished in congregational life seemed to be denied us all as children in a clergy family. In addition, in that day and time, my position as a child precluded my appealing to my parents for a more lenient approach to the situation.

Honestly, there was no mistaking that the obligatory role of participation assigned to my siblings and to me as well as to our mother made us different from others—a difference that was challenging, but not altogether unmanageable or negative. In tandem to my earlier comments about honing my gifts, I liked being chosen. I enjoyed the affirmation accorded me. I appreciated the encouragement given as in the case when I forgot the words to a vocal solo, and in another instance when the music on the piano rack suddenly tumbled down, leaving me to improvise. In both instances, the congregation was exceedingly forgiving; and the older mothers of the church responded openly, "That's okay, baby! You're alright!" I chuckle now as I recall these occasions that, as embarrassing as I felt at the time, I clearly gained improvisational skill and learned that folks in congregations can also have big hearts. Nonetheless, it can also be said that, as children, mother and we were called to the role of volunteerism and service by virtue of our being clergy family members. It was like being conscripted or drafted, whether we desired it or not.

When I later became a clergy spouse, I found that I had internalized fully the expectations of congregations about which I had become aware as a young person in a clergy family. I automatically assumed that I was to take the obligatory leadership stance in the women's, music, and educational ministries of the church. So, I took it. However, I recall an instance in one church when I discovered that there was a negotiable quality to expectations and that my biggest challenge was my own reticence to take this quality seriously. Because I had accepted a full-time position in the public schools, time and energy constraints necessitated my choosing what and how much to undertake in the congregation's life. Moreover, over the eight years of Ed's appointment to that church, we lost three babies through miscarriage. Regardless, my choice of limited involvement in the congregation was accompanied by my guilt for not being fully involved. Although I lent support to key projects carried out by the women's group and helped in the music ministry when possible, I felt guilty when it was not possible.

My sense of guilt was somewhat relieved by my ongoing leadership in the church's educational ministries. And my guilt was further assuaged in part when I could see that my clergy husband's and my affirmation of the leadership roles and abilities of the laity was matched by the laity's avowal of my diminished participation. Senior adults in the congregation were also helpful in their saying, to use the words of one, "My dear, you really don't have to do all you think you have to do." I also remember the caring response given to me by the oldest woman in the congregation as I was grieving the loss of the children. She reminded me of the scripture: "Nothing can separate us from the love of God." Her message was also very clear that God is the way-maker. My challenge became one of learning to free myself to decide what was helpful for me to do and not to do, to relinquish the burden of expectations and guilt, and to see and embrace existing supports.

Ed's Story

I will share two primary themes regarding expectations that I remember. One theme emerged during my childhood and eventually influenced my adult life as a clergyperson. The scene I remember occurred in the early 1950s. My mother, sister, brother, and I were scheduled along with our father to go as a family along with the youth choir to a well-known amusement park in southern New Jersey. The plans were well laid, and the family expectations were very high in anticipation of a wonderful and fun-filled afternoon and evening. All the laid plans and anticipated expectations were shattered, however, when my father, who was ordained clergy, told us that there was not enough room for the family. Our father said that he would have to drive the youth choir himself to the amusement park since there were not enough cars for choir members. My siblings, our mother, and I were left behind. We were deeply hurt. Anger is the proper word.

I was able to share my feelings about the experience with my dad late in his life. His response was, "Son, I was just doing the best I knew how at that time." This exchange was tremendously healing. But, back during my childhood days, the expectation was very clear. In all circumstances, the church comes first, and the family comes second. Akin to that expectation was one of sacrifice on the part of clergy family members for the sake of the members' or others' well-being. Yet, even though that childhood experience was wounding and anger provoking, in reality, it became a key governing scene in my life. It governed my own proclivity to behave in a similar manner in my later ministry and challenged me to address it.

The second theme centers on expectations regarding parsonage upkeep. I remember, for example, the expectation about the maintenance of the parsonage during my young years when my dad was pastor in the Delaware Conference of the Central Jurisdiction of The United Methodist Church. I recall that both my brother and I painted most of the parsonages in which our family lived. My role in fulfilling this task was designed as a money-saving measure for the church. While my father and mother conformed to the expectation, my father was very clear in his expectation and demand that the church pay the current minimum wage to my brother and me. I felt that this manner of handling the situation was a good compromise. It let me know that it was possible to negotiate the expectations of parishioners in the area of parsonage maintenance. But, it also raised my own sensitivities to the impact of expectations on parents and children alike in clergy families.

Of course, both our stories occurred during the forties through the early seventies which were, indeed, different times than they are today. One major difference is that, since that time, denominations and the church publications of mainline denominations have done more to recognize the importance for maintaining a viable clergy family for effective ministry. Despite this, however, the history of expectations for clergy and their families has not changed demonstrably. The challenge to confront both the congregation's expectations and the expectations that clergy family members have of themselves remains.

Vignettes of Other Clergy Families

We have already indicated in the prologue that the break up of network or village connections in people's lives today leads congregations toward unrealistic expectations of clergy and their families. It is important to state here again that the loss of contemporary relational connections between people places more and unrealistic demands on clergy and their families than in the past. In fact, clergy families are looked to today for perfect empathy when supportive care is a decreasing reality for many people.[4] Although the historical times have changed, the expectations for clergy family members remain as tenacious as they were in the past, as the following stories of clergy families show.

We are aware of a young adolescent in high school who felt like he had to fulfill the expectations of his clergy father and the church to the degree he would never wear jeans. He would dress up wearing suits, shirt and tie to go to school everyday. One Sunday, when asked, why don't you dress like us by one of his peers? He said, "I can't; I got to be like this or my dad won't like me and the church won't like me." This youth attempted suicide. Fortunately, an ongoing counseling relationship brought healing both in the youth and the family.

This case is an extreme example, and it could be easily dismissed as the circumstance of a young person who had some deep psychological problems. While this is very true, the vulnerable young man's experiences still pointed to the reality of expectations that have deep historical roots. Concerns about how the pastor and the pastor's family dress is very much part of the public expectations for clergy and their families. It has everything to do with expected public image.

In another case, an African American woman was appointed to a majority Caucasian church. This pastor had severe health challenges that required intentional self-care and attention to her own Sabbath rest during the course of each week. She faced the stereotypical view that African Americans have a relaxed work ethic and are lazy. She also confronted the contemporary expectations for pastors to be available twenty-four hours a day and seven days week that transcends racial lines. The pastor said:

> In my first church, which was African American, the senior pastor
> and I would work five days a week. This did not include Sunday. On
> one of these days we would work a half a day. My day for the family
> was Saturday, because I worked all day Sunday. In the new church, I
> worked all the time and did not take time off. When I got sick, I real-
> ized that I needed to go back to the previous pattern of taking at
> least one day off. Therefore, I put in writing my need to have at least
> one day off a week. This letter caused quite an up-roar in the church.
> They did not like the idea of me actually taking time for myself.

The clergywoman also pointed out that work expectations extended beyond her role as the pastor and included her daughter. They expected her daughter or her to care for the lawn and the exterior of the house. She said:

My daughter had responsibilities in the home, but I felt that neither she nor I had to take care of the outside of the home. She did not need to have the responsibility of mowing the lawn. I had to raise these issues with members of my congregation. They pointed out that the other pastors, who were male, took care of the lawn and the parsonage. I told them that neither my daughter nor I would do this, and I expected them to pay someone to do the tasks related to the lawn and home repair. This was a difficult time since no one had challenged this expectation of how the parsonage would be maintained.

There are also stories told of how the children of pastors are expected to be examples for other children. One pastor reported how his congregation expected his children to be examples for the rest of the kids and come to youth choir practice. He said his children were not interested in being in the choir, but this made no difference. Even though the congregation affirmed the expectations as non-negotiable, the pastor stood on his non-adherence to the non-negotiable expectation on behalf of his children. He saw his role as being a non-anxious, non-compliant presence. He said, "I chose to 'take the heat' so that maybe the 'heat' would get turned down for my kids."

One final example comes from the lament of a father who has three daughters. He complains about the grief his daughters face because they are members of clergy families:

I have three daughters, and they are constantly asking, "Why do people think we are so different and that we have to be perfect?" They complain that everybody else's children can raise hell, but they can't. They know that they are always being judged. They tell me that I am the one who was called to the ministry and not them.

The pastor stated that sometimes he wondered if his ministry is worth the grief it seems to bring to his family. His point is: "After all, when they hurt, I hurt! When they grieve, I grieve! It's hard! I don't always know what to do. I pray to God that I won't lose my kids to the church because of the stuff they bump up against. It's good, though, to have this time to get it off my chest. Maybe somebody else will have some answers."

Of course, it is important to mention that research focused on children of clergy does not necessarily show the expectations placed upon children in clergy families to be damaging. In many instances, these children take

their experiences in stride. At the same time, there are other instances
where the pressure for conformity to prescriptive behavior placed on the
children by the congregation or by the parents has the effect of "forcing"
the children to leave the church behind once they are in a position to
choose their religious path. Of utmost importance here, however, is the
key point that a clergy family is different from any other family, because
expectations of the family members parallel those placed on the one
who is ordained. We have seen in the stories above that congregations
and sometimes pastors expect clergy family members to be present and
vital contributors to congregational life by virtue of their relationships to
the pastor. Congregations look to both the pastor and the pastor's family to be perfect models of the Christian lifestyle in church and the community and to assume duties and responsibilities that foster
congregational well-being. Again, it may be said that the call of the
ordained clergyperson is transferred to family members.

What are your stories of discovering and responding to the expectations gleaned from within and outside congregations, from family members, and from yourself? As you recall your stories, pay attention to
personal strengths or positives that made it possible for you to continue
on. You will want to revisit those strengths or positives for what they
have to say for your practice of resilience on the journey ahead.
Remember that resilience of clergy family members has to do with practices that help each family member grow as a faithful Christian and to
exercise her or his calling according to the self's understanding in relationship with God. We accept the reality that clergy family members
share the call with the one who is ordained, but resilience has to do with
each family member discerning and discovering his or her unique calling from God and finding ways to exercise this calling based on choices
made by himself or herself and not imposed externally. Our own faith
bias is that internally chosen roles undertaken in response to God's call
on each clergy family member are central in the formation of healthy
identities for each clergy family member.

An Invitation to Story-Sharing

Create occasions as members of clergy families—children, youth, young
adult, and adults—to explore your personal stories of and responses to
arbitrary or non-negotiable expectations emanating from congregations,
the public, the self, or family. Likewise, disclose expectations that appear

negotiable and your responses to these expectations. You may engage in this story-sharing alone but preferably together as a family unit with or without a spiritual guide. If a spiritual guide is not called upon, a parent may lead the family unit in story-sharing following the guidelines provided in this section. Story-sharing may also take place in small groups of clergy families led by a pastoral care-giver or other experienced guide. It is critical to engage in this kind of sharing because expectations affect the spiritual, psychological, emotional, and interpersonal life of each family member. Hopeful results from exploring the expectations and the impact that they have on clergy family members include:

- a greater capacity for proactive responses building on choices and personal agency, rather than on reactive responses that result in present or ongoing anxiety;
- the capacity to discern creative, imaginative, and effective choices and responses to expectations that lead to greater personal freedom to be the self;
- the capacity to reduce the level of inner conflict and anxiety, as well as to learn ways of being a non-anxious presence when responding to expectations; and
- the capacity to undertake a variety of roles that do not conflict with or undermine one's self-understanding and self-esteem.

Unmask Your Story

During intentional occasions for story-sharing, start by simply telling your story. Whether you are alone in this process or are guiding your family in it, or are either being led by someone else or are functioning as a guide for other families, pay attention to the questions below. As a way of entering the process, story-sharers may want to reflect for a few moments on the questions and jot down some thoughts before sharing orally.

Describe the Setting

- Recall an incident or event in which you were confronted with expectations from others because you were a member of a clergy family.
- Where were you?

- Who was present?
- What was the nature of the expectation?
- What was said and by whom?

To ensure the inclusion of young children and preteens in the conversation, ask these questions:

- How do you think you're supposed to act or behave as a "preacher's kid?"
- Where did you get your ideas about how you should act or behave?
- Say something about what you have heard your parents say.
- Tell us something about what you have heard or learned form others outside the family.

Introduce the Tension or Conflict

- Talk about the inner tension you felt when you discovered the nature of the expectation.
- What was your first response?
- What were your first thoughts?
- What sort of conflicts did it produce in your thinking?

To ensure the inclusion of young children and preteens in the conversation, ask these questions:

- When somebody says to you, "You ought to act a certain way because you're a "preacher's kid," what does it make you want to do? Why?
- What goes on inside you when you hear your parent(s) or someone else say, "You're suppose to do this or that because you're in a pastor's family?"
- Do you think you're different because you are a "preacher's kid?" How? Why?

SOME CLUES

Over the years, we have told our stories of expectations appearing earlier in this chapter to each other and in small groups of clergy couples and family members who were from various denominations and lived in the same community. During the occasions of couple sharing, we discovered that prior to these groups we had never disclosed to anyone these childhood experiences of expectations. The experiences had simply gotten buried along with our responses to them. The situation of the other clergy family members was similar. We experienced permission to share. It opened the way for Anne's disclosing, for example, the tensions created around being conscripted or drafted into an obligatory role of service, and for Ed's telling of the difficult awareness of the family's being left behind in order for his dad to take other church members to an amusement park. At the same time, during our childhood, "table talk" or times of sharing at mealtimes provided opportunity for conversation around what was going on in our lives.

The earlier mentioned vignettes were shared during a clergy retreat. In these cases, clergypersons had not had prior opportunity to put into words the nature of expectations experienced by their family members. The conflict between the congregation's expectations of fulfilling church responsibilities and the clergyperson's self-care surfaced in one of those stories. Another story revealed the pressing situation of a clergyperson's standing firm on behalf of his children in opposition to the congregation's expectation of them.

Invite Catharsis

Recall from chapter one that inviting catharsis entails creating a safe space where family members feel comfortable unburdening themselves by "telling it like it is." In their moments of story-sharing, they are not judged. They do not need to defend themselves. They are free to sigh, moan, cry, laugh, or express freely the feelings that arise in the throes of story-sharing. With these reminders of the meaning of catharsis, invite family members to engage in the following:

- Describe your feelings when you were confronted with expectations. Ask young children and preteens: What words describe your feelings about being a minister's child? Or, ask: Do you feel happy, sad, angry, or simply okay when someone says to you that you need to act a certain way? What other words would you use?
- What thoughts accompanied your feelings? What did you think about saying or doing?
- What actions did you want to take immediately to do something about your feelings?

- What actions did you actually take and what was the result of these actions?
- How did you feel when you were finally able to express your feelings?

Some Clues

In sharing our personal stories with each other and with other clergy family members, Anne expressed her sense of sadness about being denied the opportunity as a youth to choose her role in congregational life and about having no recourse. At the same time, she chuckled as she recalled instances of embarrassment that were overtaken by congregational encouragement. Moreover, she recalled that her childhood experiences of expectations resulted in her adopting and acting on them in her later role as a clergy spouse. She told of her guilt as a clergy spouse for limiting her role in congregational life because of her vocational responsibilities as a public school educator.

Ed told of feeling deeply hurt and angered at the priority place of church members in his dad's actions and of his and other family members being left behind. Yet, he had positive feelings about his dad's insistence that the church pay him and his brother to fulfill the expectation for parsonage maintenance. In one of the vignettes, a youth told of pain so deep that he attempted suicide. A clergy father revealed his own grief about his daughters' experiences of unrealistic expectations. In this case, the father told of not knowing what to do, but of feeling good about "getting it off his chest" with the hope that perhaps someone else may provide some answers.

Relate Empathically

Recall from chapter one that relating empathically means listening with care to another's story and receiving the stories of others as gifts. In this light, explore the following:

- Did you find others with whom you were able to share your feelings? If so, who were they? If not, what difficulties were there in finding others or sharing with others?
- Describe the responses of others with whom you shared your feelings (e.g., would you describe them as empathetic, disinterested, affirming, helpful?)

Especially with young children and preteens, ask the questions:

- Do you feel okay or comfortable telling your parent(s) how you feel about being a "preacher's kid?" Are you okay telling us how you feel now? What would you like to add?
- Tell about a time when you felt somebody really heard what you said to him or her about your feelings. What did they do to let you know that they heard you?

SOME CLUES

During the actual childhood experiences of dealing with expectations, both of us found it impossible to express our concerns with our parents because of the prevailing views of respect to which we adhered. The opportunity for sharing came when we shared our experiences with each other and with other clergy couples. Moreover, Ed later shared his feelings with his dad and received a helpful response.

The pastor in one of the vignettes openly shared with his congregation that his children were not interested in being in the choir. Congregational members were not empathetic. Their disaffirmation resulted in his standing up for his children, or as he said, "Taking the 'heat' so that maybe the 'heat' would get turned down for my kids." In the case of another pastor, the clergy group provided opportunity for him to get his story "off his chest."

Unpack Your Story

The aim of unpacking your story is for clergy family members to assess the impact of expectations on your behavior. In chapter one we gave attention to the formation of a clergy family mythology. This mythology deals with beliefs and conviction that influence everything a clergy family member does in his or her life. Expectations held by parishioners, the public, the self, and the family influence each person's beliefs and convictions and are, in turn, shaped by beliefs and convictions. This interactive process becomes part of how and why clergy and their families act or respond in particular ways to the unique situations of clergy family life. For these reasons, it is important to explore the clergy family mythology. Before proceeding, you may wish to return to the family ministry mythology and questions appearing in chapter one. Or you may continue with the following guide designed to help you identify the myth at work in the stories already shared.

- Return to the story-telling phase where you recalled an incident or event in which you were confronted with expectations from others because you were a member of a clergy family.
- Review the incident and the internal conflicts that this event had for you.
- Recall the feelings that emerged both during the incident and as you shared it.
- Recall whether or not you had support in expressing your feelings.
- Try to assess the influence that the conflict had on who you are. For example, did you conform? Did you rebel? Did you try to put on a public face while trying to hide your private behavior? Did you come to grips with the expectation and find creative and imaginative ways to handle the expectation?
- Once you have identified the approach you took in response to the expectation, assess the impact that this approach has had on you, others in your life, and on your views toward and involvement in ministry or congregational life.
- Name the convictions and beliefs that developed as a result of your assessment. Use a metaphor, image, or concept to capture in a few words the nature of your beliefs and convictions (e.g., is your metaphor, image, or concept focused on the perfect model? Getting along or going along? Settling? I did it my way!)
- Name the plotline that is at work in your conviction and beliefs about expectations. For example, is the plotline tragic or hope filled? Does it enhance your ministry or take away from it? Does it facilitate your growth and the growth of others, or does it hinder your growth and that of others?

Some Clues

Our experiences of expectations during our childhood had profound implications for our forward journeys. We both developed high expectations for ourselves. When we married and became a clergy family, we both had to wrestle with our tendencies to comply uncritically with the expectations of congregations. We recognized that as children, we did not have a choice in our responses except to comply. As adults, our wrestling had to do with our recognizing that our forward journey need not be governed by our childhood responses to expectations. One of the ways we brought a balance to the congregation's and our self's expectations was to affirm the abilities of congregational leaders to carry out tasks they assigned to us. But, among the most helpful approaches along the way has been our intentional engagement in story-sharing with others. In those times of sharing, we were able to develop what we call a "good enough" plotline. Central to this plotline is our view that the myth of perfection had to be wrestled with and that we had to move on with the belief in our own worthiness before God and our affirmation of our "good enough" effort before God.

In the vignette of the youth who attempted suicide, a positive plotline became possible as the result of the family's intentional engagement in counseling. In another vignette, a pastor's approach was clearly one of rebellion against the congregations' expectation of his children, whereas another pastor found hope in sharing his story in a group setting from which answers from others could come.

The Way Forward

Recall from chapter one that moving forward has to do with assessing your plotline in light of the plotline of faith. An important part of the assessment process is identifying some biblical stories, texts, theological or doctrinal foundations that help family members evaluate the plotline of their story. On this basis, explore the following:

- What Bible story or text helps you evaluate or look critically at the beliefs and convictions you hold? How do your beliefs and convictions guide your responses to expectations? How would you answer the question: What in your beliefs and convictions makes room for God's acting in your life in ways that give you hope and direction in confronting difficulties with expectations? What in your beliefs and convictions makes room for your experiencing God's promise and guidance?
- Does this evaluation lead you to update, downgrade, discard, embrace, edit, or re-author your beliefs and convictions about how you see and respond to expectations?
- What steps do you need to take in the future to help you handle the expectations that you confront?

SOME CLUES

The concluding part of Anne's story highlights the wisdom of an elderly sage on which she has relied over the years. The verse, "nothing can separate us from the love of God," evoked in her a critique of her underlying belief that her compliance with the expectations of others was needed and, in fact, a pre-requisite for her to be loved by them. Her movement toward a "good enough" plotline was not based on her earning the love of others by being the "perfect" respondent to their expectations of her. Rather, Anne's plotline was based on awareness that in the face of disappointment or criticism for not desiring or being able to meet others' expectations, there is a love—the love of God—that transcends this human condition.

As Ed was sharing his story, he realized that his father gave him a blessing on which to affirm a powerful conviction. For Ed, the blessing was a spiritual symbol not only in the form of profound empathy given by his father, but also in the form of a divine blessing from God mediated through his father. At his father's funeral in 1999, the symbol of Elijah passing on his mantle of leadership to Elisha was apropos for his relationship with his father. All of Ed's life, his father was the religious leader for the family and the extended family. Ed was always unwilling to pick up the mantle of being the prayer warrior for the family, in part because he was rebelling against the expectations of others for him. At the funeral Ed realized that his father had waited to die until Ed picked up the mantle of prayer warrior for the family. Ed told the congregation that he prayed for his father while his father lay sick in the hospital. This was the first time Ed had prayed for his father while in his father's presence. The next day his father died. Ed told the congregation that he finally realized that his father was waiting for him to take on the leadership of the family so he could die.

Ed had finally overcome his personal ministry mythology. He was no longer fighting the expectations of others or of his father. He was free to fully embrace what God had in store for him in his ministry. On the day of his father's funeral, he embraced whatever God had in store for his future. In fact, he looked forward to the ministry that God would give to him. He was ready to move forward.

Tips for Engaging Young Children and Preteens

In the process of story-sharing, it may become all-to-easy for young children and preteens to become silent partners. Make every effort to ensure that they are not left on the sidelines, lest we foster their feelings of abandonment and convey that their very real experiences as clergy family members are unimportant. Children need nurturing interaction, not only between adults in the clergy family, but also between them and their siblings. It is important, then, to ensure opportunity for them to talk, express their feelings, as well as to think through what they are experiencing, imagine what they would like to see happen, and contribute to suggestions for problem-solving and the journey forward.

Importantly, children learn that they are included in family sharing not simply during specially chosen occasions for story-sharing, but through how the family relates on a daily basis. From our own journeys as children in minister's families and based on others' currently on that journey, we offer a few additional tips:

- Recognize the moods and attitudes of children and unhesitatingly ask: Are you okay? Is something bothering you? Let's talk about it.
- Observe the interactions between your children, as well as the children and adults in and beyond the congregation. Also, where there are siblings, observe how they interact with one another. In response to your observations, you may create opportunities to describe a situation that was positive or one that raises concern. Encourage your child to share what they experienced. As parent(s), you may ask open-ended questions such as: "What else would you like to say about it? Can you say more?" It is helpful, too, for you as parent(s) to interject supportive language such as: "I'm glad that you have fun with the friends you have made." Or, "It must be hard for you to be in this new situation." These kinds of conversations should always include some discussion with the child about what is needed in follow-up.

CHAPTER THREE

Moving

"Nothing ever ends without something else beginning or begins without something else ending. Perhaps this would be easier to remember if we had a word for it. Something like 'endbegin,' or 'beginend.'"[1]

"Clergy move! That's a fact," a pastor said. "Sometimes I'm ready for it. I mean, it signals a new opportunity. Other times, I'm not sure it's the right thing to do, even though there is no option to remain where I am. In still other instances, I don't have time to really think about it. One day, my feet are firmly planted in one church. The next day, I'm packing up. Sometimes I just find myself saying, 'God surely has a sense of humor.'"

The pastor continued, "Of course, if the whole matter of moving involved just me, that would be one thing. But, it gets complicated where my family is concerned. I would like to say that it is easy to take my spouse's and my children's feelings and needs into consideration. That's not always the case. Inevitably, there are those 'no choice' moves. Most of the time, taking it in stride is the way we as a family have been able to do it. But, honestly, that 'taking it in stride' sometimes happens only after my spouse or my children make a few pointed statements when a new move is announced: 'You've got to be kidding!' or 'We're going *where*?' or 'I'm not going!' And honestly, I can name a time when the whole family literally went 'kicking and screaming.'"

Moving is one of the aspects of clergy family life that is often tough. And, particularly with regard to its impact on families, many pastors today wonder whether the sacrifices that family members make for the sake of ministry is worth it. The many stories about moving told by pastors in and beyond itinerant polities are often punctuated with cries for guidance on how to respond to their families who are often hurting. This chapter focuses on a process of sharing clergy family stories associated with moving and of exploring ways to address the challenge of moving. Our intent in the story-sharing process is to look for signs of the winds of promise in the form of patterns of resilience that have already carried clergy families through experiences of relocation and that can yet carry families through these experiences. We will seek to uncover in our story-sharing not simply helpful approaches to facing the trauma of moving, but also ways of moving with hope beyond an ending in one place to a beginning in another place.

With reference to moving, we define resiliency as the clergy family's capacity to imagine both the gains and losses in relocation, as well as to find helpful ways of responding to the realities of loss associated with being uprooted and transitioned from one church to the next. Resiliency is built by cultivating practices that enable each family member to deal with moving in positive ways. With regard to clergy families the basic practice is related to grieving and accepting the inevitable.

A key element in the process of story-sharing is also the effort of the story-teller and story-listener to discover the plotline supporting the stories that are told, because patterns of resilience will often emerge in the plotline. This discovery of the plotline means that we will invite story-sharing in order to look at patterns of behavior that have occurred in past moves, present concerns about moving, and thoughts about anticipated future moves. Moreover, we will invite reflections on the nature of the social contexts involved in the relocation experience and the range of inner feelings associated with not simply the relocation experience, but also the sharing of that experience. Our constant questions will be: "Where have we already experienced the winds of promise in the experience of moving? How may we anticipate, move directly into, and discover hope that the winds of promise bring us in the experience of moving?"

As a way of beginning, we will provide a perspective on the nature and consequences of moving. Following this setting of the stage, Ed will share part of his story of moving from his childhood to teen years in his clergy family. In his story-sharing, he will reflect on the impact that the threat of moving had on family members including himself. Anne will also tell aspects of the impact of moving on the family during her father's itinerant ministry. Brief attention will then be given to others' stories. Through these stories, we invite you to reflect on your own stories of moving in preparation for entering into a guided individual or family story-sharing process.

Perspectives on the Nature and Consequences of Moving

Clergy families who are in itinerant polities and those who are not move at some point in the ministry journey. Yet, there seems to be greater expectation of and less choice in moving in itinerant systems found, for example, in Methodism. Indeed, according to Robert Kohler and Mary Ann Moman, itinerancy was a strategy for mission for early Methodists.[2] However, originally, itinerant ministry was undertaken successfully by single men who were able to freely move about their circuits, because they had no family demands.[3] Over time, itinerancy became the experience of both unmarried or single clergy and families who moved from place to place in accordance with the clergyperson's appointment by a Bishop. Clearly, though, regardless whether clergy families are in itinerant systems or not, moving evokes a wide range of feelings from excitement, great anticipation, and a new or renewed sense of hope to sadness, feelings of rejection, and anger. For all, moving is an uprooting experience and has tremendous consequences for family members.

Even though the pastor and family members may look forward eagerly to relocation, by its very nature, moving means leaving a place where a sense of home has been established and connectedness with others in church and community have been forged. Likewise, even when that home and connectedness were not all a family desired, there is always something or someone that makes leaving either difficult or bittersweet for somebody in the family. Indeed, clergy family members tell of a number of reasons that raise anxiety and even anger in them when they are faced with the possibility or reality of moving to another location:

- I don't have any control over the situation. I feel looked over and left out;
- I feel like a "trailing" spouse. And that's not all. I'm losing my job and the loss of salary and benefits that I fear will not be replaced;
- I'm concerned about the schools in the new town;

- Our youngest child says, "I like my school. Why do I have to leave?" Our teenager says, "I'll simply 'die' if I have to leave my friends. It's my senior year!";
- We're used to our doctors and like the medical care we receive where we are now. It's not going to be easy leaving that comfort zone;
- I'm a single parent. I dread the task of finding suitable daycare and other help I need for my children when I must be away from home;
- I'm concerned about safety in the neighborhood to which we are to go.
- It's common knowledge that, where we are going, the parsonage leaves much to be desired;
- We're going to a church that has had fourteen preachers in ten years. It's not a comforting thought that the "revolving door" may already be turning before we get there; or
- The pastor before me was there for twenty years. I worry that the congregation is in grief over the departure of their beloved pastor or whether they will be joyful to receive me as their new pastor.

Although some clergy family members may find helpful the ritual practices of departure celebrations given by a congregation and welcoming ceremonies provided by a new congregation, other family members may not deem them useful. For them, these events may trigger or exacerbate deep feelings about moving that may, in fact, go unaddressed once the event is over. Some new or alternate forms of rites of passage may be needed. In fact, family life cycle theorists infer this need.

According to contemporary studies on the family life cycle, the events of birth, the onset of puberty, marriage, mid-life, old-age, and death are no longer the universal marks of life transitions for which there is need for rites of passage of some kind. More specifically, contemporary studies identify nodal points as new additions to the life cycle. A nodal point is an analogy taken from astrology and refers to the point of intersection of two great circles in the celestial sphere where new realities emerge. For contemporary family life cycle theorists, for example, geographical uprooting is a nodal point or event signaling the onset of new realities for persons. The theorists point to this nodal point as having great significance in contemporary life.[4]

Nodal events are not biologically determined and, therefore, differ from the traditional life cycle transitions such as birth, the onset of puberty, marriage, mid-life, old-age, and death. According to Betty Carter and Monica McGoldrick, nodal events are not complete life transitions. In the case of the traditional life transitions, people move through well-defined stages and crises associated with them on the basis of a biological "pull." But, nodal events seem to center on a disruption of the natural biological flow.[5] The latter seem to be more about loss, and the movement toward healing is not so predictable. In this regard, the reference to geographical relocation as a nodal event is of particular importance in our focus on clergy families. Carter and McGoldrick confirm that, as a nodal event, geographical relocation can have severe outcomes for family life, especially when family members leave an emotionally important house or community. They add:

> What is also crucial is the extent to which [geographical location] changes the balance of a marriage. For example, if it takes a wife further away from her mother, it can either free her or lead her to become more dependent. In general, it might be said that such uprooting, to the extent it takes a couple further from one's spouse's extended family and closer to the other's, will shift the balance, though not necessarily always in the same direction.[6]

Importantly, the inclusion of nodal events in the currently available body of literature helps us understand better the experiences of loss resulting from events such as geographic relocation. While this life event does not move forward with the force of biology, the human spirit is resilient, and recovery and healing are possible. There are practices that uncover and build resilience and that contribute to recovery and healing. While it is clear that moving can have a devastating impact on clergy family life, it is possible for the family to respond with creativity and imagination. There is an increasing reservoir of practices for building and maintaining resilience in the face of moving. A key process for entering into these practices is story-sharing. Thus, we will move now to sharing aspects of our own stories of moving in advance of inviting your engagement in story-sharing.

Ed's Story

Itinerancy was a dominant conversation between my parents every year prior to annual conference, where decisions about clergy appointments were made. From my perspective as a child, the whole subject of moving appeared troublesome especially because, in those days, we never knew whether we were moving until the last act on the last day of each annual conference, which was the bishop's reading of clergy appointments. This way of handling appointments evoked a view that decisions about moving were arbitrary. For our family, especially my mother, it fueled a sense of having no control over our lives.

Both my parents were college graduates. My father was seminary educated. For a period of time following my mother's graduation from the University of Pennsylvania, she had been a social worker in the city of Philadelphia, Pennsylvania. After some time, she became a teacher and later a guidance counselor in the Philadelphia Public School System where she remained in the same school for twenty-seven years until her retirement. Despite my father's serving churches in three different states, including Pennsylvania, New Jersey, and Delaware, my mother managed to remain at the same school for the entire twenty-seven years. Somehow, my father was able to negotiate with the bishop and superintendents his move to communities where my mother could take public transportation to work. At no time was my father appointed beyond thirty miles from the city of Philadelphia while living in three different states. Nonetheless, severe anxiety emerged in our household in anticipation of annual conference where the possibility of our moving was a reality given the way appointments were made.

The nature of the anxiety became manifest in my mother's extreme agitation with my father, whereupon he would withdraw from her emotionally. This situation heightened the tension in the home. In my own mind, I imagined that my parents were getting ready to split up, and the family that I knew would be no more. For a month or two, the tension and anxiety in our home was unbearable for me. Thus, I became preoccupied with my parents and their relationship. I had a very hard time focusing on my own specific childhood age-related tasks. Even today, the anxiety I internalized as a child resurrects as I recall what took place ritualistically every year around the appointment process at annual conference time. I can say that it was fortunate that my father had long pastoral appointments over many years, and when we did move, my mother's career was not threatened. Clearly, my fears and my mother's fears were anticipatory ones. Nonetheless, I developed a low tolerance for change that related directly to the tension in our home around the threat of moving. I internalized the family anxiety, and this internalization led to my fear of loss of one parent due to divorce. Annual conference and the appointive system on which itinerancy is based became too much for me to handle.

During my childhood, I remained silent about what I observed, heard, and experienced surrounding the issue of moving. I did not approach my parents or anyone about the situation of moving or my own anxieties about it and how my parents were handling it. Children were simply not part of the conversation in that day and time. My effort to come to grips with the impact of itinerancy on my family and on my personality did not begin until 1965 when I entered Boston University School of Theology. Upon entry to the seminary, one of the first tasks for all students was to take a battery of tests including one to establish a psychological profile called the Edwards Personal Preference Test. When the scores on the test were interpreted to me by one of the pastoral counseling professors, one score stood out above all others. My score on tolerance of change was very low. At the invitation of my interpreter, I enthusiastically "dove into" exploring the reason for such a low score. During that exploration, I discovered that not only was my fear of change an issue, but the way I handled my anxiety was also problematic. I wanted to help my parents resolve their own anxiety and help them stay together. I rebelled by refusing to learn to read until the eighth grade. My refusal had the effect of rallying both parents to address this problem. Unconsciously, I was seeking to keep them together by rallying them around a common problem—me.

As an adult, I was also able to have a conversation with my father about my mother's anxiety. He told me of an instance quite early in his ministry when my mother was pregnant with my sister. At that time, my brother was nearly three years old and I was almost two. My father recalled that my mother was elated about a promised forthcoming move to a larger church. This move was deemed a positive one because the salary from my mother's continued employment would not be needed and she could complete the pregnancy and be at home with the three children. However, the appointment to the new church was reversed on the final day of the annual conference. Instead, my father was sent to a small church with a meager salary for the expressed purpose of bringing healing to a congregation that had experienced a gross indiscretion of their pastor of several years. This pastor was appointed to the church promised to my father. The surprising turn of events soured my mother's attitude toward itinerancy. Her sadness and anxiety persisted throughout my father's ministry and her negative attitude toward itinerancy remained up to the time of her death. Nonetheless, she never refused to move and would say, "I'm just going along with the program."

When I asked my father how he dealt with his seeming wrongful treatment and the whole matter of moving, he responded by reminding me of the story of his call, which I had heard some years before. He ended by saying that he pledged to go where he was sent. He was also very clear in stating that God called him to a ministry to fulfill. He ended by saying that the words of the Apostle Paul spoken in front of King Agrippa had been his words throughout his ministry and would always be his testimony: 'I was not disobedient to the heavenly vision'" (Acts 26:19).

As a result of my father's sharing the story with me, I was able to understand the history behind the anxiety and tension in the family as well as to learn my father's perspective on moving. Particularly regarding my mother, the story helped me to see that every year she actually relived the pain of betrayal she felt. My father's sharing also shed light on why mother was adamant about my not entering the ministry and expressed great disappointment when I entered seminary and was ordained. An important insight I gained from my father was that feelings and behavior always have a context and that it is not always possible to discover in fullest measure the reasons for them immediately. When I asked my father how he dealt with moving, he told the Genesis story of Abraham and Sarah who were called by God to leave the comfort of their home with only a promise. He said that, for him, God always keeps God's promises to us no matter how long it takes, and that he moved forward according to that belief. His sharing with me also awakened in me the reality that there are opportunities to seek answers to trauma that besets us or those we love. It is important to look for and enter fully into those opportunities.

Anne's Story

A powerful scene has remained dominant in my memory of my dad's first appointment. It was to a church in a small town in Indiana. In advance of the final decision, the church, which had not had a full-time pastor for a while, invited us to visit. We also went by the parsonage. The day of the visit was a stormy one in which rain came down in torrents. With every mile, the situation seemed to grow worse and, as we drew near the church, mother blurted out, "I don't know about this!" Only a few people showed up at the church, but they were nice enough, as I recall. We were guided to the parsonage, which sat on the edge of a creek. When we entered it, mother gasped at its sparseness and the dampness that penetrated every room. As we left and moved down the road, the wheels of the car slid into a mud-filled ditch. One of my three younger brothers opened the door on his side of the car, immediately stepped out, and began to cry, whereupon the rest of us kids—four of us—followed not fully comprehending that we were stepping into mud that quickly covered our shoes.

It took all of us together—mother, daddy, and five kids—to push the car free. We climbed back into the car wet and grubby with mud and drove back to the place that had been home for a number of years. Anxiety was written all over mother's face and body. Of course, now, it is nothing short of hilarious recalling that scene of seeing our feet and shoes disappear in gooey mud and hearing our parents' words of encouragement as we tried to move the car forward, "Okay children, let's pretend that we're Popeye the sailorman." But, it was not funny then.

Ultimately, we did not go to that church. We moved instead to a church in Ohio, where we remained for one year before moving again to another church. The experience in Indiana served as a marker event for what became a ritual of anxiety preceding these two moves in Ohio and every subsequent one.

It was not a matter that mother was adverse to moving. She had openly said that she was willing to go wherever dad was sent. A key part of her anxiety, felt by all of us, seemed to stem from uncertainty about when and where we might be moved and about the nature of the new place and the people in it. There was also an established "folklore" about congregations and cities or towns about which clergy families became aware. It included clues about possibilities and pitfalls of being appointed to a particular church or place. Awareness of this "folklore" increased mother's anxiety, especially when it highlighted concerns about safe environments, schools for us, and options for her to work. She often dealt with her anxiety through music. She was an accomplished pianist and singer; and on occasion, her disquiet about moving resulted in her private time of singing, "Sometimes I feel like a motherless child, a long way from home." Sometimes our whole family would come together around the piano and sing. Mother would say that this is a way of releasing the troubles of the day. She also found personal meaning in the psalmist's words, "How could we sing the Lord's song in a strange land?" (Psalm 137:4) Yet, for her, singing was precisely a way of seeing that she and the family could make it a little further, or as she would say, music was our letting go and letting God."

My dad was not wholly unaffected by the prospect of moving or an actual move. He always wanted the best for his family and I could see that he felt any concern or pain mother or children felt. The depth of his own feelings was most often expressed in his prayers during family meals for God to sustain us. Also, from time to time, presumably in response to a whole range of concerns, he could be heard throughout the house singing one of his favorite hymns, "When the Storms of Life Are Raging, Stand by Me." Apart from dad's response to the itinerant ministry, each of us children responded in our own way. One of my three younger brothers was most affected by the move from the first church in Ohio to the second one. He had just finished the first grade where he had bonded with children both in the school and community. His sadness lasted for an extended period after the move and his adjustment to a new school was difficult. It is interesting that this brother, along with one other brother, actually chose military vocations that required them to move about. The same brother later entered itinerant ministry.

As for me, there was always something about moving that was intriguing. In fact, this perspective on moving stayed with me as I moved three times in my own vocational life before marriage and then eight times with Ed after our marriage. Of course, moving did not always proceed without problems, and it was difficult leaving those I came to love. Nonetheless, I welcomed what Robert Frost called "the road not taken." Moving from place to place also matched what I called my sojourner's theme, based on the words of a song, of going on "to see what the end will be," and my question, "I wonder what another place might be like?" To this day, I can't quite explain why that is so, except that my parents once said that I have wanderlust or longing for the perfect place. My siblings' response to my stated views about moving was simply, "You're weird!" Someone else once suggested to me that perhaps that first experience of possibly moving to the wet, muddy place in Indiana set in motion my continuous search for what I consider the perfect place.

Dad actually remained for nearly ten years in each of two appointments before becoming a district superintendent. Although the anxiety connected to the possibility of moving each year never abated for my mother, another emerging part of her journey was grief for leaving what became familiar to her and for those who became cherished friends. After each of the lengthy appointments, her expression of loneliness became quite pronounced and she fought depression until she gained a sense of comfort in her new surroundings and a close network of friends with whom to relate. Her period of greatest loneliness came during dad's years as superintendent, when all the children were grown and she and dad were empty nesters with no real sense of a single identified "congregational home." Mother's situation was difficult for me because I wanted to do something to alleviate her loneliness but lived too far away to have any impact on a daily basis. Although at one point mother said it was something she alone had to come to grips with and deal with, I felt deeply her pain and had to reckon with my own sadness provoked by my inability to help her. Writing, phone calls, visits, and praying became my only means of intercession on her behalf.

Vignettes of Other Clergy Families

In the prologue, we told the story of the crisis in the clergy family brought about by the move of the pastor during the spouse's difficult pregnancy and delivery. In that situation, the ability to carry out the move was facilitated by the pastor's and his spouse's confession of the difficulty and pain of their circumstance, their belief that they would be able to survive the difficulty of moving, and their reliance on God's help to see them through it. As in our personal stories, the stories of other clergy families are not always as traumatic as the one told in the prologue. Nonetheless, the impact of moving on the family unit is still pronounced.

In another instance, the pastor felt strongly that it would be in the best interest of her children to remain in her current associate position for a while longer. She said that her need to communicate her concern was great and that she was intentional about expressing it to her superiors. Looking hindsight, she said that she had no regrets sharing her position and her desire, even though in the end, she was appointed elsewhere to a position as senior pastor. The new situation has remained "rocky" for her school-aged children. Prior to the move, she recalled one of her children saying, "None of my friends is moving. Why do I have to move?" Moreover, members in the church expressed difficulty in accepting a woman as pastor. But, she maintains that her memory of her call to ministry guided her move and keeps her going. She remained steadfast that moving will not deter her carrying out that call. Her words were, "I can't give up! God called me, and I believe God didn't bring me this far to leave me." She also said that she accepts responsibility for being a strong presence and guide for her children in order to assist their adjustment to the new church and to ones that will come in the future. She said, "My hope is that I can do something to make a difference for their sake."

What are your personal experiences as a pastor and as clergy family members of anticipating, preparing for, and actually moving from one church to another? As we indicated in the previous chapter, it is important to disclose painful experiences. However, it is equally necessary to give attention to the positive ways in which you and family members have dealt with moving. Thus, as you recall your stories, pay special attention to personal strengths or positives that made it possible for you and family members to move from one location to another. Revisit those strengths for how they may assist future experiences of relocation. The following section is designed to guide you through the story-sharing process.

An Invitation to Story-Sharing

The story-sharing process to which you are invited here will follow the same format provided in the preceding chapter. Again, you may engage in it alone but preferably together as a family unit with or without a spiritual guide. Or, story-sharing may take place in a small group of clergy families led by a pastoral caregiver or other experienced guide. The format will again include an invitation to tell your story, engage in catharsis, relate to others empathically, unpack your story, and explore ways of moving forward.

In the last chapter, we emphasized the importance of including children in the story-sharing process. Their participation is important because they have their own real feelings, anxieties, and concerns about moving. They adjust to moves in different ways and need opportunities to share their experiences and imagine with the help of adults ways of making a positive transition come alive.

Unmask Your Story

Whether you are alone, guiding your family in story-sharing, being led by someone else, or are functioning as a guide to a clergy family group, allow stories of moving to surface. The following questions are designed to assist the process of sharing orally or by writing brief responses on paper first, if it is deemed helpful, and then by sharing orally.

Describe an Event of Relocation

- Recall either your first experience of moving or particular experience(s) of moving that you found positive, exciting, problematic or difficult.
- Name the church(es) from which you moved and the church(es) to which you moved.
- In what locations were the churches and what was the distance between them?
- Recall what happened as you and/or other family members learned about the move(s), your preparation for the move(s), and the actual experience of leaving one place and arriving in the new place.

To ensure the inclusion of young children and preteens, ask them the following:

- What do you remember about what happened when we moved the last time? Or, what do you think would happen if we were to move?
- What did you leave behind when we moved? Or, if we were to move, what would you leave behind?
- What did you take with you when we moved? Or, if we were to move, what would you want to take with you?
- Tell a story or draw a picture of a house we lived in the past. Include the people you remember, things you remember about the church, or things you remember about your school.

Introduce the Tension or Conflict

- Talk about any personal concerns that arose in the process of learning about the move(s), your preparation for the move(s), and the actual experience of leaving one place and arriving in the new place.
- What concerns were raised for you that you felt would be difficult

to resolve? Did you voice your concern to anyone? If so, to whom? What was the response? If you did not voice your concern to anyone, why not?

- What awareness did you have of concerns of other family members about the move(s)?

To ensure the inclusion of young children and preteens, ask the following:

- What was the hardest thing for you about moving? Or, what do you think would be the hardest thing for you if we were to move?
- As you left your old home, church, or school, was there anything about leaving that made you cry? Say something about how you felt or feel now.
- What were you thinking when you moved into your new home, church, or school?

Some Clues

For Ed's family, every move was problematic because of the anxiety it evoked in his mother. But, one particular move was especially difficult. In that instance, an anticipated and acceptable move was reversed and the family was thrust into a less satisfactory one. The turn of events embittered Ed's mother and heightened Ed's fear that his parents' marriage was in jeopardy. He remained silent about the tension he felt deeply because children were not typically included in what was considered adult conversations. Ed's opportunity to tell and process his childhood story did not come until he was an adult. His hindsight view uncovered not only his need but also his actions designed to address the family breakup he feared.

Anne recalled the first aborted move of the family and the anxiety it caused, especially in her mother. She also remembered a move that was extremely difficult for one of her brothers who had become attached to friends and the school he attended. She shared her own idea that moving had some excitement attached to it, even though her view was not necessarily the accepted one in the family.

One of the vignettes revealed the circumstance of a pastor whose move was difficult not only for her children but also for her because of the reticence of church members to accept a woman as pastor. One of her children made the comment, "None of my friends is moving. Why do I have to move?"

Invite Catharsis

Ensure a safe space for family members to share more fully experiences of moving and their feelings about it. Making a safe space possible happens as every family member is invited to talk and reveal their points of view and feelings in their own way and time. The opportunity for children to share their thoughts and feelings is particularly important because of the impact that moving and the parental responses to moving have on them. Use the following as guides for further recall and the exchange of thoughts and feelings.

- Say more about your experiences of moving that you omitted earlier.
- Describe the thoughts and feelings you had at the time of the move(s) you described.
- Describe the thoughts and feelings you are having while telling the stories of moving.
- What did you do about your thoughts and feelings at the time of the move(s)? Explain what you did and why? What was the result of your action? Or, what did you want to do about your thoughts and feelings, but didn't? Explain what you wanted to do but didn't do. Tell why you didn't act on your thoughts and feelings. What was the result of your inaction?
- Especially with young children and preteens, ask: What words would you use that capture your feelings about moving, (e.g., sadness, fear, anger, anticipation, excitement, etc.).
- With what statements do you identify on the list included earlier of reasons that raise anxiety or anger when family members are faced with the possibility or reality of moving? Why?

Some Clues

Ed described the tension and anxiety evoked by moving as unbearable. He also told of his later discovery of his development of an intense intolerance for change. Ed's story continued with his awareness after he became an adult that he had refused to learn to read during his childhood out of his desire to bring his parents together around a common concern—him. Moreover, his conversations with his dad shed helpful light on his mother's thoughts and feelings of anxiety and sadness.

Anne's own expressed viewpoint about the excitement of moving was not transferable to other family members. Their responses were encapsulated in the expressions, "weird," wanderlust, or her search for the "perfect place." During the later years of her parents' itinerancy and Anne's adulthood, she discovered that issues connected to her parents' moving did not escape her. She became concerned about her mother's loneliness and had to deal with her own sadness evoked by a sense of impotency in alleviating her mother's circumstance. Because she lived at a distance, her way of addressing the situation was through calling, writing, visiting, and praying.

Recall in the reflections of the pastor that opened this chapter that there were occasions when faced with moving, family members said: "You've got to be kidding! We're going where? I'm not going!"

Relate Empathically

A range of feelings will likely emerge in the process of sharing stories of moving. As a result, it is essential that persons are listened to with care and without judgment, affirmed in their sharing or reticence to share, and encouraged to vent their feelings as fully as they can. In this process of relating empathically, use the following as a guide:

- What difficulties were there in finding others with whom you could share your thoughts and feelings during your experiences of moving?
- How important was it for you to be able to share your thoughts and feelings with someone during your experiences of moving? Why? What difference might it have made in your circumstances of moving?
- What difference does it now make that you have shared your story?
- With children or pre-teens, ask: what would it be like if you could not tell your story to anyone? What else would you like to say?

Some Clues

Ed told of remaining silent as a child because, in that era, it was not the place of children to enter into was deemed as adult conversations. The interpreter of the inventory he took upon his entry to Boston University became a healing presence because of the insights about his family's responses to moving he was able to glean during the interpretation sessions. During Ed's adulthood, his father also became a healing agent because, in conversations with him, Ed learned of the history behind the tension and anxiety in the family surrounding moving.

In one of the vignettes, a pastor told of the importance of sharing her concerns about a move that had the potential of affecting her children negatively. She expressed her concerns to her superiors about moving and her desire to remain in her associate position and did not regret doing so, even though the final decision of her superiors was to relocate her.

Unpack Your Story

The purpose of unpacking stories about moving is to gain a clearer picture of your particular thoughts and feelings about and responses to moving, and to begin to see evidences of resilience to affirm and build on. More specifically, gaining a clearer picture requires an evaluation of the self's experience(s) of moving. As in the preceding chapter, the mythology that frames what it means to be a clergy family in general and a member of that family in itinerancy in particular often plays a role. Beliefs and convictions about being in clergy families who are subject to relocation can provide clues to how clergy family members actually view experiences of moving. These beliefs and convictions also function as building blocks for family members' plotline or view of clergy family life in the throes of moving. The plotline may contain images that reflect a tragic orientation to life in the throes of moving, or it may reveal a hope-filled orientation that can either facilitate or hinder family members' moving forward into the winds of promise. The following guide is designed to help you in this exploration.

- Return to the story-telling phase where you recalled your experience(s) of moving.
- Review one or two aspects of your story that generated the most energy or emotion. With young children and preteens, simply ask: What was hardest for you to talk about?
- Recall the most intense thoughts and feelings that emerged both during the experience(s) of moving and your telling the story. With young children and preteens, ask: Is there something more you would like to say about what made you sad, afraid, angry, ready to go, or excited about moving?

- Explore what it means to you to be a member of a clergy family who is subject to move as the result of the decision of someone outside the family or by the choice or pressure of a clergy family member. What impact does this membership have on who you perceive yourself to be or want to be?
- Use a metaphor, image, or phrase to capture in a few words the nature of your beliefs or convictions about moving (e.g., God never promised me a rose-garden; when you're given lemons, make lemonade; you can take a mule to the water, but you can't make him drink; for every end, there is a new beginning; I'm going through).
- Name the plotline that reflects your convictions or beliefs about moving. For example, is the plotline tragic or hope-filled? Does it enhance your ability to continue on as a member of a clergy family, or does it hinder this ability?

SOME CLUES

The most intense part of Ed's recall was his renewed feeling of unbearable anxiety and fear of family breakup because of the trauma surrounding moving. His anxiety had been prompted by his mother's longstanding embitterment set in motion by her experience of unfair treatment in the moving process. Even so, she developed a plotline that allowed her to move anyhow as exemplified in the words, "I'm just going along with the program." These words framed her ability to be resilient in the midst of disappointment.

Being a member of a clergy family was not easy for Ed and he also got a clear impression from his mother that becoming a minister was not a valued vocational identity. Yet, the plotline Ed embraced was a more hopeful one. The trauma of moving that dominated his family life did not deter his response to his call to ministry. The phrase, "Moving is traumatic! But, I'm going through!" became his means of embracing a future and forming a resiliency that would help him confront uncertainties that lay ahead.

In Anne's story, the potential move to her dad's first church prompted her mother's words, "I don't know about this." Although these same words were not repeated with every subsequent move, they functioned as a guiding metaphor for her mother's plotline of hesitancy with regard to moving. However, the presence of resiliency in her plotline was revealed in her use of music as a release of the negatives of moving and the embrace of the next step. Anne's plotline included Robert Frost's poetic metaphor, "The road not taken," and the words, "going to see what the end will be." The resiliency is captured in these phrases. She formed a plotline of expectancy in which the future was seen as open.

In one of the vignettes, the pastor's phrase was, "I can't give up!" This image in the face of moving reflects her resilience and formation of a hopeful plotline centered on constancy or steadiness and endurance amidst the challenge of itinerancy.

Moving Forward

In this section you are invited to explore your plotline and resilience that come into play in the throes of moving in light of a plotline of faith. Central to this exploration is an uncovering of biblical stories, texts, theological, or doctrinal foundations that help sustain family members in responding to challenges of moving. On this basis, explore the following:

- What Bible story(ies) or text(s) help(s) you to evaluate or to look critically at beliefs and convictions you hold about moving? How do your beliefs and convictions guide your responses to moving? How would you answer the question: What in your beliefs and convictions makes room for God's acting in your life in ways that give you hope and direction in confronting difficulties in moving? What in your beliefs and convictions makes room for your experiencing God's promise and guidance? Be sure to include the children. Especially ask them to say something about what they hear that helps them and gives them a sense they will be okay in moving (e.g., see the story, "Pack Your Bags, Boys, We're Goin' to Egypt" or "Land o' Goshen!" a children's story based on the story of Joseph's family in Genesis 45:16-46, found on: http://www.essex1.com/people/paul/bible-stories-to-egypt.html).

Also see the story of Abraham's move in Genesis 12.

- Does this evaluation lead you to update, downgrade, discard, embrace, edit, or re-author your beliefs and convictions about how you see and respond to moving? Invite especially young children and preteens to brainstorm everything they can think about that can make moving pleasurable, in spite of their finding it hard to move.

- What steps have you taken in the past that have helped you handle the moving process and concerns connected with moving? What steps do you need to take in the future to help you handle concerns about moving?

SOME CLUES

The biblical passage that guided Ed's dad throughout his itinerant ministry was the statement of the Apostle Paul after he told of his conversion experience during his defense before King Agrippa: "After that, King Agrippa, I was not disobedient to the heavenly vision" (Acts 26:19). This scripture framed the conviction of Ed's dad that, no matter what, he was committed to being faithful to his call.

Anne's mother drew from the psalmist's words to frame her own hermeneutics of suspicion prompted by the challenge of moving. The psalm helped her raise her own burning question when moving to a new location: "How could we sing the Lord's song in a strange land?" (Psalm 137:4) Implicit in her calling on this lament was her own feeling of being a captor in the itinerant system and her attempting to find an answer to this sense of captivity. Being able to frame the question functioned as a means of opening the way for her to, in essence, "sing anyhow," as a means of "letting go and letting God."

Tips and Resources for Families with Children

Resilience is built and maintained as clergy families recognize the varying ways moving affects family members and then enter into the kinds of approaches we have suggested here to help them see and realize positive transitions. Where children are concerned, it is especially important to be aware of their reactions to relocation and include them in processes through which they learn ways of addressing experiences of moving that are difficult or painful. In addition, creating family rituals are important ways of traversing the journey of relocation. These rituals might include the following:

- *Create a family historical resource.* With young children, create a family storybook at each new location into which the adults and children make entries at designated times (e.g., monthly, or at the time of special events, activities, or key experiences). To craft the storybook, children and adults together draw pictures, include photos family members take, and write or print thoughts, feelings, and expectations upon moving to a new place. Thereafter, include new thoughts, feelings, happy times and moving experiences, disappointments, difficulties, and concerns. When relocation becomes a possibility or reality, review the storybook for the feelings and meanings it evokes and for talking about what is important to take into the new place and what is to be left behind. End the storybook with ideas of what you will do to "blaze a trail of hope."

- *Develop family talk times.* Mealtimes provide opportune moments to share with one another the events of the day and conversations around thoughts, feelings, and concerns about moving that arise both when a move is suspected or imminent, and when there are worries about or desires to move.
- *Plan pre-move strategies.* Take family trips to the new location. Visit the schools prior to moving. Explore safety rules for the new city. Explore the positives of moving, but also realize and focus on the losses and the power of prayer that allows for lament and opens the pathway to hope.
- *Ensure nurturing moments.* Nothing can replace reassuring words and daily hugs that say to one another, "We care about one another. We love one another. We're in this journey together."

Although designed for schools, two resources on relocation are helpful ones to adapt for use with young children and preteens, ages 9-12 in clergy families. The resources are also available in Spanish. They include: *Let's Make A Move! A Creative Visualization Book for Young Children* and *The League of Super Movers: My Moving Adventure,* a full-color book for preteens, both published by BR Anchor Publishing, 2044 Montrose Lane, Wilmington, NC 28405-6208.

CHAPTER FOUR

Making Family Life Count

A family is like a forest; when you are outside it is dense; When you are inside, you see that each tree has its own position.1
—An Akan Proverb from Ghana

Chapter two emphasized a process for clergy families to recognize, build, and maintain resilience when facing public, family, and personal expectations. Chapter three provided a framework and guide for clergy families to explore the challenge of moving and the nature of resilience, creativity, and imagination already existing in the family and yet needed to undertake this challenge. These chapters also laid some groundwork for the challenge of making family life count. That is, imbedded in the stories of clergy families are struggles to make family life count and how to respect and give priority to the needs of family members and family life in the face of expectations and the disruption of repeated moves. But, other concerns must also be considered in making family life count. Time and sensitivity are needed to give adequate attention and response to issues connected to family size and make-up, the age/stage of each family member, and the family's life cycle. Especially through each age/stage, children in clergy families require parental attention, including from the clergy parent. Building and maintaining resilience happens through attention given to all of these aspects of clergy family life.

The reality is that making family life count is often difficult given the

time intensive responsibilities of clergy resulting from both congregational and denominational demands. Many clergy and clergy family
members are quick to say that making family life count is hard! Some
confess that this quality of life is simply non-existent! But, it is also true,
as we said in the prologue, that there are clergy families who successfully meet the challenge of making family life count. However, these
families also confess that doing so requires intentional and straightfor-
ward effort. This chapter is about our private lives as clergy families and
our discovery of ways we already use or may yet use to honor and give
priority to family life. Specifically, the chapter will guide clergy families
through a process of story-sharing to uncover, assess, and form ways of
creating time and space to respect and give priority to family. We will
focus as well on family beliefs and convictions that foster positive
growth of each family member and on what we call "family Sabbath
time," which is time for simply being family together and forming and
renewing family bonds.

Resilience here is defined as the capacity of the family to function as
a coherent unit with consistent support for each family member's com-
petent negotiation of challenges associated with life transitions. Life
transitions include:

- individual life cycle events such as moving from childhood to
  adolescence, from adolescence to young adulthood, from young
  adulthood to adulthood, from adulthood to middle adulthood,
  and middle adulthood to older adulthood;
- events associated with singleness especially with reference to
  unmarried clergy, the marital life cycle such as mating and formation stages, early marriage stages, middle marriage stages, and
  older marriage stages;
- family life cycle stages such as the expansion of the family with
  the birth of children, the contraction of the family with the leaving of children and the post-parental years;
- transitions associated with losses and the threats of loss and how
  families respond to them such as the death of family members
  and illness; and
- nodal transitions, to which we referred in chapter three. These
  transitions expand beyond geographical relocation discussed in
  that chapter to include divorce, remarriage, and retirement.[2]

The story-sharing process in this chapter opens the way for you to reflect on any of the aforementioned aspects of life transitions. But, special attention will be given to the transition of children in clergy families from childhood to adolescence and young adulthood. This emphasis stems from consistent, deep concerns raised by clergy families in workshops we have done about difficulties of making life count and the impact of this reality on the children, especially as they move in and through adolescence.

The Significance of Problems of Youth and Young Adults: Vignettes and Follow-up Responses

Stories abound that bear the strain of families' efforts to make family life count in ways that help children in clergy families thrive in their process of growing up. We will share two brief vignettes here and a brief personal family story. At the same time, we want to place the struggle in a broader social-cultural context, because there are issues in this wider milieu that contribute to the challenge of clergy families to make family life count.

A Case Study

The topic was the need of clergy and clergy family for Sabbath time. There were about thirty pastors, including one bishop and six district superintendents, attending a clergy retreat. The bishop conveyed his view of the importance of pastors taking time out for relaxation and renewal. In fact, the Bishop reported that when he was pastor of a large, multiple-staffed urban congregation, he required clergy staff to take one weekend off every seventh weekend for Sabbath rest. There was one requirement, however. On the off Sunday he invited the clergyperson, spouse, and family to sit together in one of the three services. He indicated that his goal was to be practical about increasing the morale of his clergy staff. He spoke about the success of this innovative approach to family self-care, and about the increased productivity of the staff resulting from the endeavor. What also evolved from the families' experiences was their appreciation for the sanction to enter into the needed Sabbath time. One comment by the Bishop stimulated a lot of commentary from the group of thirty pastors. He said that he wanted to make sure that the children of the clergy staff did not grow up hating the church. His point was that many clergy spend most of their time dealing with the needs of the church and not spending quality time with their families.

The bishop's remarks led to many pastors sharing their feelings and fears about their children and how the children felt about the church and the fact that one (or both) of their parents was a pastor. One pastor told of a time when his seven-year-old daughter called him on the downstairs phone in their home and asked for "an appointment with the pastor." He told her to come upstairs. When she did, he asked her why she needed an appointment. She said this is what she heard his congregational members ask when they needed to talk to the pastor. His daughter obviously felt neglected. She wanted and needed time with him. This pastor told of how this experience hurt him. He spoke of how his guilt over the experience was compounded by another development. His twenty-eight-year-old daughter refuses to go to church because of her experience of the church's preventing her from having a father.

Following the pastor's heart-tugging story-sharing, other members of the group began to tell stories related to their children. One story came from a pastor whose children were alienated from the church. He spoke with profound emotion and concern about the harm he felt being a pastor had caused his children. He used the metaphor of Simon, the Cyrene, who was compelled to carry Jesus' cross (Mark 15:21; Matthew 27:32; Luke 23:26) to capture what he envisioned being a pastor meant to his children. He wondered how the life of Simon the Cyrene turned out after being forced to assume a role in which he had no choice. For him, the role meant being drafted as an innocent bystander into a drama of someone else's creation, which in the long run had the potential of being destructive to the one being conscripted. He used this story as a metaphor for children who are forced to take on the expectations and roles of their clergy parents when they have no say in it. And, the fact that children are allowed to carry the load without needed support makes the situation all the more poignant.

Affirmation emerged from the group that being asked to carry another person's cross is a helpful metaphor for children in families where one or more parents are ministers. Being a child of a clergyperson is not a role that children knowingly choose or seek. It may also be said that spouses of clergy do not always choose or seek their role in the clergy family. Like children, they may have a great deal of difficulty carrying what for them is akin to a cross. Some feel it is too much to ask.

Before directly addressing the need for making family life count, it is imperative that we explore the nature of family life in contemporary culture and its adverse effect on clergy families. Following this brief excursion into contemporary culture the task will be to examine the unmasking, catharsis, relating empathically, unpacking, and moving forward dimensions of making family life count.

A Personal Family Story

We have had abundant opportunities to recall our own stories of relating as a couple and to reflect on our relationship in group contexts. Here, we want to share brief aspects of that story in conversational form along with some reflections.

In times of looking back, we have readily confessed that there was no mistaking the time and energy demands of Ed's responsibilities as pastor, urban minister, and doctoral student during his early ministry years in Massachusetts. In Ed's words, "I had difficulty balancing my work outside the home with commitments to spending quality time with my wife, Anne." In the prologue we revealed some aspects of this difficulty with making the family of creation a priority. We also told more of his story in chapter two when, in his childhood, a trip to an amusement park was denied because of the priority given by his father to the transport of church members. In his words, "The early phase of my marriage was captured by my beliefs and convictions that family had to come second while my ministry came first." Thus, Ed spent most of his energy doing his ministry.

Anne recalled: "I became really concerned about Ed's time away from home and by his unspoken view that I must simply understand the importance of his ministry involvement. I had real feelings about it. Of course, I knew and was reminded by him that his work schedule was difficult. Outside of the family, his work actually included his local congregation, a position with the local council of churches as an urban minister, taking one course a semester in a post-seminary degree program, and role as a trainee in pastoral counseling at a local pastoral counseling center. That was a lot! And, I wanted him to succeed in his role as minister and to support that success in whatever way I could. Honestly, I also knew before we married about the time intensive demands placed on clergy based on my own childhood in a clergy family. Nevertheless, regardless of my wanting to support my husband's success and knowing the demands of clergy responsibilities, being on the receiving end of it as a spouse was still hard. It seemed that there were no words to convey what I was feeling."

Ed's viewpoint was: "I actually felt that I was doing a fairly good job of balancing my work outside the home with spending quality time with my wife. But, things changed drastically when Anne became pregnant. The pregnancy was complicated, and I had to commit more time to my relationship with Anne than I had anticipated. This thrust me into an internal crisis. Even so, I realized much later in my life that I had not revised my personal convictions about the priority of home life, and I actually continued all the activities outside the home with too little modification. Honestly, I gave only minimal attention to Anne's needs." Anne interjected: "He did try to address the difficulty we were having in response to my sharing entries in my diary, not only about how I felt as the spouse of a clergy and my desire for his success, but also my need for his presence and more time together."

On reflection, Ed confesses: "It was not until mid-life that I finally got the relational messages that caused me to set aside my convictions and beliefs that made ministry a central priority over family life. In fact, it was not until I had major heart surgery in 1994 that I finally understood the importance of balancing family life with ministry and the appropriate role of self-care as central to my physical health. I learned that I had been running from intimacy up until mid-life, and this fear of intimacy was the major contributing factor in the clogging of my heart arteries. My recovery from heart surgery and living healthily for the rest of my life required me to commit to the practices of intimacy and making my relationship with Anne a central priority." In short, it took Ed's brush with near death to force him to revise his ministry convictions and beliefs, or what is called his ministry mythology.

The message we both want to convey here is that commitment to family life and to the growth of each member in the family will not only maintain the health of the minister. It will also make the pastor fit for ministry. The bishop in the illustration cited earlier in the chapter is correct. Commitment to family is essential for the self-care of the minister; it is also essential for effective ministry.

Another Clergy Family Story

We had an opportunity to hear the stories of a clergywoman and her teenage daughter while engaging in a conversation about children, congregational expectations, and the parents' role in clergy families in the lives of their children. The clergywoman began her story by recalling a situation in which she uprooted her daughter from familiar and comfortable surroundings by moving to a new congregation. Her daughter agreed that being uprooted was the right word because she had been well connected with her peer group where she and her mother had been for a number of years. Both the mother and her daughter agreed that all of these relationships and connections were disrupted by the new move. The daughter also indicated that she was not necessarily adverse to moving, but she wanted some "space" to deal with it in her own way and on her own time. She made this view plain especially because the church members seemed to want her to become fully immersed in congregational life right away. The daughter described this situation as different from what had happened previously and that she felt the members were being "too pushy," and not respecting her as a person.

Thus, the story of the pastor and her daughter was framed by the mother's situation of raising a teenage daughter in a new congregation to which they had recently moved and the daughter's dealing with it in a way that was comfortable for her. And, at the center of this story frame was the reality that, more than ever before, the teenage daughter needed support from her clergy mother, and the mother needed to accept responsibility for making family life count for her daughter. This twin task was pivotal for both of them in light of the relocation and new expectations.

This scenario unfolded on how the pastor attempted to create a home atmosphere where she could negotiate between what she expected of her daughter, what her congregation expected from her daughter, and how the daughter understood her own self to be. The mother had to discern the appropriate age-related behavior for her daughter and support her daughter's emerging self, despite the congregation's expectations or her expectations as a parent. The mother said she wondered if she was equal to the task. However, she said that a driving force for her was the importance of her relationship with her daughter and her daughter's well-being. Even though fulfilling her call to ministry was central to her, she did not want to sacrifice her daughter in the process or to alienate her daughter from the church.

The pastor said: "I could see that the move to the new church was initially traumatic for my daughter. I was aware, too, that she was quite different from the youth in the new church. The members in the new church also expressed concern because they thought my daughter was too withdrawn and disconnected from the church. This concern of the parishioners caused me to become more observant of my daughter's behavior. Frankly, I concluded that there was nothing wrong with my daughter. In fact, I concluded that my daughter was demonstrating self-confident behavior, and the parishioners had misread her cautiousness. Also, I felt that she should not feel obligated to become part of the youth group unless or until she was ready. So, even though my daughter was her own unique self, she was like any of the other youth in the church with a right to decide whether she wanted to attend."

The pastor continued: "What I observed as a mother was the willingness of my daughter to engage anyone who approached her. What the parishioners observed was her not initiating conversation or engagement with others. She waited for others to take the initiative in conversation and engagement." In continuing the conversation, the daughter said: "I'm an observer. So, on Sunday, I sat in the back of the church and just watched people as they came in and what they did during the service. Sometimes, I took a book, because I like to read and I would read while I watched." Her mother interjected: "Yes, and I mentioned to her that it wasn't a good idea to bring and read a book during the service." The daughter then replied: "She was right. I got the message and I stopped the book reading. But, I still sat in the back and watched what was going on. I told you I'm an observer. I wanted to see what the place was like and how the people act so I could get an idea how I would fit in. I think people kept observing me too to see how I was going to act as a preacher's daughter. They still do, I think. Things have gotten to be okay, though. I've found some friends. It's not such a bad place."

The mother also talked about her daughter's need to engage her. They both spoke of having ongoing conversations that have been helpful in adjusting to the new church and new home. The daughter was willing to engage her mother with what was going on inside her. In these intentional times together, the mother also gained increasing awareness of the new emotions with which her daughter was struggling. And she was able to affirm her daughter's need for space to handle the new feelings without being pressured by the church members' expectations. Together, they were able to talk about the sadness each of them had for what they had left behind in the previous church; and they shared what they saw as good signs in their new location. Their conversations were helpful ways of affirming family ties.

In their times together, the mother and daughter told of how the mother expressed pride in her daughter's maturity. She expressed confidence that her daughter was really growing and developing into a very unique and responsible individual. The mother said, excitedly, "I just praise God that she has confidence in herself in this difficult situation." Her excitement was evident as she continued her reflection on her daughter's apparent resilience or her capacity to face challenging situations head on and with growing maturity.

She went on to say: "I am not sure where this confidence came from, but I think it came from the time when I was in seminary. She was a child of about seven or eight years of age at that time. She was well known on the campus. She was right there with me when I attended classes. She also developed a relationship with students and one of the male teachers who would speak with her before and after class." The mother felt that her being on the seminary campus and building relationships with a variety of persons fostered her daughter's independence and ability to handle difficult situations. She concluded that it was during the seminary experience that her daughter learned to engage adults and to enter into conversations with them with confidence. From her perspective, this experience also made her daughter secure in herself in the face of intimidating expectations of others.

She also admitted that, in the throes of the situation, she hoped that she played an important role of modeling for or teaching the church members about ways of affirming persons' uniqueness and responding to age-appropriate expectations of youth. She said, "I hope they could see that my daughter's behavior was normal, not just for her, but also for other teens within the church. Of course, I'd be the first to say that it is not easy meeting the needs of the congregation, the needs of my child, and my own needs. But, I know for sure I'm not going to let my child down."

Comments on the Socio-Cultural Context of Contemporary Family Life

Two key socio-cultural issues impact family life today including the power of modern technology and the commodification of human worth. Modernity evolved from the impact of rapid and unrelenting technological advancement on contemporary life following the industrial revolution. Commodification is one of the results of modernity where human worth and value are determined by the market place, rather than through one's relationships with other human beings and one's connection to faith communities. The effect of valuing the market place over human relationships reduces human worth to a commodity to be bought or sold.

Sylvia Ann Hewlett and Cornel West highlight the impact of technology and commodification on contemporary family life. They alert us that a pervasive emphasis on marketing values that reduces human identity and relationships to a commodity undermines the accent on essential qualities of caring, nurturing, and cherishing needed to carry out family life and good parenting. The emphasis on marketing values is all the more disastrous because these essential qualities are receiving less support from social structures, especially the media and government policies that determine the parameters of family functions.[3] They state, "When parents are so seriously disabled that they cannot perform their central functions, the results are disastrous for our nation—and the fallout on children is quite lethal."[4]

In their analysis, the parent role is eroding and the web of care is breaking down. Children are being born without the loving support of parents and a supportive community. They trace this abandonment of children by contemporary culture to public policy and private decision-making and the impact these dimensions have on the non-marketing values of care, nurture, and cherishing. They contend that big business, government, and wider culture wage an undeclared war on parents, and that market values are crowding out family space, making it difficult for family life to count. They state the following:

> Small wonder, then, that parenting is a dying art. Small wonder,
> then, that parents have less and less time for children. And time is,
> of course, at the heart of the enterprise. Being a "good-enough" par-
> ent requires providing a child with gifts of love, attention, energy,
> and resources, generously and unstintingly over a long period of
> time. It involves nourishing a small body, but it also involves grow-
> ing a child's soul—sharing the stories and rituals that awaken a
> child's spirit and nurturing spiritual bonds that create meaning and
> morality in the child's life. The Greeks had a name for it: they called
> this cultivation of character and virtue in a young person *paideia*.[5]

Clergy families are not immune to the cultural pressures that place marketing values higher than the non-marketing values needed to make family life count. Yet, clergy families are caught in a double bind. On the one hand, clergy families are like all other families in that we feel the call of the marketplace and the need to pursue what society values as important. Yet, on the other hand, we are expected to perform and exemplify the non-marketing values of care, nurture, and cherishing not only within our own families, but also for many other families beyond our own as noted in the chapter on expectations. Yet, children in clergy families desire and need the nurture, care, and cherishing that is essential to their growth and development. When these qualities are lacking or insufficient, children even in clergy families suffer. When we crowd out non-marketing values, we create an environment that forces children and youth into pre-mature adult responsibility of not simply caring for themselves, but often for their parents. Role reversal is perhaps one of the major effects of neglecting the practices of care, nurture, and cherishing, especially when there are no surrogate and family substitute options. One of the major causes of children of clergy abandoning the church is the feeling that one must sacrifice one's real relational needs for the sake of the church.

Despite the double bind, clergy families must find a way to make family life count on at least three different levels. The first level is creating time to engage in story-sharing for purposes of discovering what family members are thinking, feeling, and going through and for discovering the presence or need of forming or re-forming resilience. The second level is dealing with what is called "the ideal family portrait." This portrait particularly regards the parent(s) ideal image or expectation of how children should behave and grow up in a minister's family as well as the child's self-understanding and expectation of her or his behavior and maturation. The third level pertains to the family's intentional adoption and welcome of Sabbath time, including the formation of family rituals through which bonding, resilience, and joy of being family are furthered. In the next section, we begin to explore practices of making family life count. We invite you to engage in story-sharing primarily around parents and children in clergy family life.

An Invitation to Story-Sharing

This section provides a guide for clergy family units or small groups of clergy families to engage in story-sharing that focuses on the three levels mentioned above. In following the guide, we suggest that times be designated for small groups of parents to share their stories with one another and for older children and adolescents to enter into a separate time of story-sharing. However, it is important that individual clergy family units create occasions for both parents and children to enter openly together in conversation with or without a guide. The intent of these conversations is to center on stories that uncover the thoughts, feelings, and experiences of both and the need especially for support of children. Additional attention may also need to be given to the relationship of the marital dyad in clergy families.

The second level of foci on the ideal clergy family is a particularly important and complex one in making family life count. For that reason, some prefatory remarks need to be made in advance of your entering the story-sharing process. Specifically, as means of making our private lives as clergy families count, it is helpful for us to explore and examine the beliefs and convictions that we have about the kind of home environment needed in order for each family member to grow into his or her full possibilities as children of God. Especially with regard to our children and youth as well as to spouses, making family life count relates to our ideal images of family, of children and youth as they grow and develop within our clergy families and ideal images of spouses.

With particular regard to the ideal family and child images, it is our conviction that there must be intentional family time together. Moreover, the family environment must take into account that, optimally, there is an inevitable interaction between the parent's expectations and the child's own emerging self-understanding and expectations. However, the environment in which this interaction occurs should be such that it produces maximal growth and development of the child. It is neither the parent's expectations nor the child's self-understanding that should be the focus; rather, it is the quality of the interaction. For example, the parent's expectations for the child's growth and development should be age-appropriate based on the child's maturational needs. This means that parents need to be attuned to the child's life cycle, developmental needs. Thus, as the child matures, his or her self-understanding will become more prominent in the parenting role. Early in the child's growth and development, the parent's expectations are internalized, and as the child grows older, these internalized expectations become the maturing child's self-expectation. As the child matures through adolescence into young adulthood, the original parental expectations are uniquely fashioned by the budding adult into his or her own identity.

With regard to the marital dyad in clergy families, there must be awareness that each partner in the marriage will likely have an ideal image of what the mate should be like. These images may be quite disparate, and, therefore, in need of negotiation or revision. It is also important to note that these images will typically have a bearing on the adult and child relationships in the clergy family.

Unmask Your Story

At this juncture, we invite your individual clergy family unit, on your own, or small groups of parents, and separate groups of older children and youth led by an experienced guide, to build on earlier conversations (see chapter two). Get in touch with your ideal image of how children in a clergy family should behave and grow up. The story of these expectations should begin at a particular point in time. The story telling into which you are invited will reveal your hopes and aspirations for the child according to age/stage. The story-sharing should also include what the parents and children believe is essential to giving children support in navigating their role as children in a clergy family. The intent is to discover what actually takes place and what is needed to make family life count for the children.

Describe Your Ideal Image of Being a Member of a Clergy Family

- Begin by inviting family members into story-sharing about family time together and about how each member came to know ideal ways of behaving as members of a clergy family. If you are in your individual family unit, be sure to invite the children to be part of the story-sharing. Have some paper or newsprint and pencils or markers on hand for some sharing in written or picture form.
- When and in what setting(s) does your story take place? As a parent, what did you do or what happened that moved you to inform the child(ren) about family time and ways to behave or grow up as clergy family members? As a child, what happened that gave you ideas about family time together? About how to behave or grow up as a clergy family member? At another time, marital partners in the clergy family may share stories focused on occasions of learning each other's views of how to behave as clergy and

spouse within and outside the family setting. In a group setting, single unmarried clergy may share stories revealing views communicated by extended family members or fictive kin (friends who function like family) on how they should behave as clergy.

- Allow each parent and child to list key words describing their views of family time together and about behavior that emerge in your stories. Young children may draw pictures. In a group setting, single unmarried clergy may also complete this exercise.

Introduce the Tension or Conflict

- As family members, describe as fully as you can any concerns, disagreements, or conflict that arose as part of the story you told about family time together and ways to behave as clergy family members.
- Each family member may share an additional or follow-up story revealing concerns, disagreements, or conflict arising from family views about behaving as clergy family members.
- As the parent(s), summarize the level of tension or conflict between your ideal image of your child's behavior and attitudes. More precisely, is there a conflict between your ideal image and the child's self-understanding about who she or he is? Also, summarize tension or conflict around family time together.

Some Clues

For Ed, the primacy of church, community, and school over the home was learned from his experiences early during his childhood in a clergy family. He did not become fully conscious immediately of his carrying out his ministry in this way; and he did not question it, even though, as a child, he had deep feelings about the experience of his father's preferential attention to church members. Ed deemed his approach to carrying out ministry to be ideal behavior. Tension surrounding his ministry schedule surfaced especially during Anne's pregnancy.

The pastor and her teenage daughter each had a story about their move to a new church and home, including the mother's awareness of uprooting her daughter and the daughter's desire for "space" to deal with it. Both had to confront their ideal images of what was or was not appropriate behavior, including the mother's image of how her daughter should behave in church; the mother's image of her "right" behavior to deal with her daughter's behavior and the church's attitude; the daughter's self-view of her own behavior; and the daughter's view of her mother's response to her. Tension surfaced especially around the daughter's self-perception of her differentness from the youth in the new congregation and the church members' assertion that she was too withdrawn. At the center of the daughter's story was her expressed need for space to approach the situation in her own way—that is, by being an observer—and the mother's wrestling with how to care for her daughter's needs. The story pivoted on the daughter's need for support from her clergy mother and the mother's acceptance of responsibility for making family life count for her daughter. The story revealed the mother's concern about whether she would be equal to the task of negotiating the daughter's self expectations, congregational expectations, and her expectations. Through this expression, she showed feelings of inadequacy.

Invite Catharsis

This time of catharsis will focus on three areas of sharing within individual families or in clergy family groups where separate groups of children and adults or small groups of both children and adults meet. First, create opportunity for family members to share in depth personal thoughts and feelings about the ideal images of being and behaving as clergy family members already described in the story-telling part. Second, allow family members to explore additional aspects of their stories that pertain to ideal images of behaving as clergy family members they have not already shared. Third, say something about the presence, need, and of availability of family time to explore and negotiate views about behaving as clergy family members as well as simply being together. The following guide is designed to assist this time of sharing:

- Each family member may explore what family means and thoughts and feelings about the views expressed in their own and others' stories. Allow every family member to tell what they would place highest on their list of ways of being and behaving as members of a clergy family at this point and time. To stimulate conversation, ask family members to answer the questions: What makes us a family? How do I think I am supposed to behave as a clergy family member? Also, ask family members to respond to the following: I would really like to know more about how you think I should behave as a member of a minister's family. Be sure to allow sharing of thoughts and feelings about what is heard.

- What opportunities are provided for simply being together, for family fun times, and for sharing stories, thoughts and feelings with one another about images of behaving as clergy family members? When and where do they take place and who makes them happen? What happens during these times and how do you feel about what happens? If these opportunities are few or non-existent, explore why this is so, and what you would like to happen.

Specific attention should be given by parent(s) to the following:

- Discuss the extent of the nature, time, and frequency of family gatherings and outings. List the kinds of gatherings, such as watching TV, family games, movies, sporting events, plays, concerts, dinnertime, picnics, vacations, school events, church functions, and others.
- Discuss the extent to which your child(ren)'s behavior meet(s) your ideal image? Pick a particular event that illustrates how the child has either conformed to or conflicted with your ideal image.
- Think about the child's self-understanding and his or her actual age-appropriate developmental needs as best you can. To what extent would you consider your ideal image of your child(ren)'s behavior realistic according to their actual age/stage or developmental needs?
- If the child's self-understanding is age-appropriate, how do you support him or her?
- If the child's developmental needs are not age-appropriate, how do you respond to the child so that his or her needs could be age-appropriate?

During this time of catharsis, spouses may also explore more fully present images of each other's behaviors, any changes in those views over time, how or whether those views have been discussed, and emerging feelings about the views and responses to them. Be sure to tell additional stories that illustrate the nature of the images and responses to them connected to your age/stage or your family's life cycle stage.

Single pastors may also share more about their own ideal images of the self's behavior as clergy as well as the nature and especially the impact on them of images emerging from or communicated by family members such as parents, siblings, and fictive kin (friends who function like family). Consider your age/stage.

SOME CLUES

Anne told of having "real feelings" about the time intensive demands of Ed's ministerial role that took away from family life. She added that she had an image of Ed's success and knowledge of what went into achieving it, while at the same time, she confessed that the situation of minimal family time was still hard.

The story of the clergy mother and her teenage daughter revealed the mother's feelings of inadequacy or of not being "equal to the task" of negotiating the daughter's image of her own behavior, the congregation's image, and her own image. Yet, she overcame this feeling because of the importance of her relationships with her daughter and her daughter's well-being. Pivotal in the story was the mother's disclosure of her image of her daughter's behavior according to what she knew of her daughter's adolescent needs for "space" and her image of her own parental responsibility in light of the daughter's critical need for support from her mother. While she supported her daughter's need to be herself, she didn't shy away from communicating what she felt was inappropriate behavior, which was received by the daughter as an appropriate action.

Relate Empathically

This section concentrates on how well we think we are attending to our child(ren)'s and one-another's feelings. Making clergy family life count involves taking seriously our child(ren)'s and one another's feelings as well as affirming and appreciating one another for who the self is and for risking sharing the self's innermost thoughts and feelings. When we welcome the thoughts and feelings of family members, we give them a sense of caring, nurturing, and cherishing that are essential in contemporary family life amidst the impact of technology and commodification. A variety of approaches may be used in this aspect of the experience of shared story as means of further easing self-disclosure in this unfolding process. These approaches may include persons' preparing and sharing a poem, song, rap, picture, journal entry, or movement or dance to express themselves. Use the following guide to assist this time of sharing:

- Family members may add any thoughts, concerns, or feelings that have not already been shared about ideal images of a family and of behaving as members of clergy families.
- What have been the most helpful times of sharing your stories, ideas, and concerns about what it means to be a member of a clergy family? Where has this sharing taken place? Who has been part of this sharing? Who initiated it?
- What barriers have there been to sharing your stories, ideas, and concerns about what it means to be a member of a clergy family? Say something about how the barriers have developed.
- Decide on some ways to affirm family members' presence in your family. Carry out the experience of affirming them. Also decide on some ways to show appreciation for persons' involvement in this story-sharing process. Enact your show of appreciation.

Some Clues

The mother not only attended to her daughter's inner struggles, but she also paid attention to her daughter's feelings. The daughter had feelings of loss, and she needed the space to process them as well as the engagement of her mother as she processed these feelings. The daughter was able to express how she felt, and she told her mother that she was all right. Both mother and daughter spoke of family time for expressing depth of feeling, and especially the mother's affirmation of and pride in her daughter's ability to handle the situation.

Anne told of the helpfulness of sharing entries in her diary about her feelings related to being the spouse of a clergy, the time intensive demands ministry placed on Ed, and her need for his presence.

Unpack Your Story

At this time, we turn our attention to evidences of resilience in the journey of being members of a clergy family. Underlying this focus is our view that clergy family members have developed inner personal resilience or the capacity to negotiate or move through challenges related to being a clergy family member that has not been identified. The process of story unpacking is designed to discover this resilience. However, we stated in the beginning of this chapter that resilience of clergy families or the ability of these families to function as a coherent unit with support for each members' functioning forms when respect and priority are given to the needs of family members. The intent in unpacking your story is to uncover how, where, when, and with whom your family has dealt with issues of being clergy family members and your family's plotline or views of what is needed to move forward together into the winds of promise. Use the following guide to assist your exploration:

- Return to the various parts of your story you have told in this chapter about being a clergy family member. Highlight one or two key aspects of your story that generated the most energy or emotion.
- Recall the most intense thoughts and feelings that emerged, both during the time of the experience that reminded you of your membership in a clergy family and as you told the story.
- Summarize what it means to you to be a member of a clergy family with requirements of behaving in a certain fashion. Reflect on your age and stage.
- What have been the most helpful ways you have dealt with troubling aspects of being a member of a clergy family with requirements of behaving in a certain fashion? List these ways on paper.
- What would you say are some ways you now behave as a member of a clergy family that require change? Negotiation? Why? What is needed to alter your views of your own behavior and other family members' behavior? How may behavioral changes be handled best? Why? Share your feelings about what has surfaced in the discussion. Summarize your thoughts on paper.
- Name the plotline that reflects your convictions or beliefs about being part of a clergy family and about requirements to behave in a certain fashion. Is the plotline tragic or hope-filled? Does it enhance your ability to continue on as a member of a clergy family, or does it hinder this ability?

SOME CLUES

Here, we want to focus on the story of the clergy mother and her teenage daughter. Much energy emerged around the mother's excitement about her daughter's self-assuredness, growth, and resiliency along with her recall of seminary as a place that contributed to her daughter's formation of resilience. When the mother resisted the parishioner's call for the coerced engagement of her daughter with them, she affirmed the right she had as a parent to support her daughter by protecting her from what could be harmful to the daughter's growth and development. The mother made clear that, even though each teen is a unique individual, adolescents in clergy families are no different from other teens when they are learning to be separate selves from others. Clergy families need to provide a buffer zone for their teens to grow as normal teens.

This single pastor was not simply demonstrating a nurturing and healthy practice of connecting with her daughter. She learned that by doing as she did, she was also modeling or teaching the adults of the church how to appropriately engage the youth of the congregation by the way she related to them about her daughter. She taught them by her responses to them that her daughter was neither disconnected nor aloof. Rather, she taught them that her daughter was being an age appropriate teenager who would connect with them when she was ready. She told the parishioners that this was normal behavior not only for her daughter, but also for other teens within the church.

She also recognized that her role as pastor and parent was not easy; and she reminded other clergy parents that it is not always easy to set aside the expectations of church members with regard to the developmental needs of children or youth. Through her clarity that she was not going to ignore the needs of the family for the sake of ministry, she exposed her conviction or belief in the necessity of balancing family and congregational life. The family plotline was a hope-filled one centered on making family life count. The nature of both her resilience and her daughter's emerged in hindsight as they told of their ability to stand up for what was important to them with a sense of rightness about it and based on their convictions about the importance of family life.

The Way Forward

The way forward entails clergy families' formation of beliefs, convictions and practices that make family life count, and that assist the family to respond to the age appropriate needs of each family member. In this final part of the story-sharing process, our purpose is to engage families in exploring practices that contribute to ongoing efforts to make family life count, including assisting family members in moving through age and stage-related transitions. As in previous chapters, we invite your attention to biblical stories, texts, or theological foundations that may further assist your efforts. We recommend that adults and children come together for this time of sharing. Therefore, in your individual family setting, or in small clergy family groups of both adults and children, explore the following:

- What Bible story(ies) or text(s) help(s) you evaluate or look critically at beliefs or convictions you hold about being a clergy family member? About being at your particular age/stage or family life cycle stage?
- What in your belief or convictions makes room for your experiencing God's promise and guidance?
- Does this evaluation lead you to embrace or change in any way your view of being in a clergy family?
- Create a story of what you believe to be the best way for members in your family to care for one another. If you are not the clergy in your family, what especially would you want the clergy in your family to do to make family life count? What do you see and are willing to carry out as your part in making family life count? If you are the clergy in the family, what is especially important to you to do now to make family life count? What will your family do together for Sabbath rest?

SOME CLUES

In the case study earlier in this chapter, a pastor recalled the biblical story of Simon the Cyrene to capture his view of his children's role as clergy family members.

The pastor's selection of the story suggests, too, that clergy bear something of a "cross" in their role as family members by bearing the weight of multiple demands that cause stress and, yet, require appropriate and helpful balancing of family and church life.

The same case study referred to time created for clergy to take one weekend off every seventh weekend for Sabbath rest. On Sunday of this weekend, the clergy, spouse, and family sat together in the church service. Underlying this practice is the view that Sabbath time is a period when we enter into God's presence for sustained conversation with God through prayer, fasting, and discernment. Moreover, we can be on sabbatical with others where we engage in worship and reflection through sharing what is taking place in our lives. Clergy and their families who recognize how important family life is to the work of ministry can make covenants with each other to periodically set time aside for sabbatical leaves for worship and reflection on making family life count.

Sabbatical leaves are essential primarily because there are social pressures within the church, as well as in culture, that work against relational values. Therefore, it is impossible for clergy families to sustain relational priorities without periodic retreats and sabbatical leaves. Making family life count, then, is a major effort that must extend beyond the individual family. We have learned from clergy families that their involvement in workshops where significant story-sharing and support occurs functions as Sabbath time. Thus, this form of Sabbath is important. It is also a way of building family resilience by providing opportunities for clergy families to join ranks with other clergy families, learn from one another, and enter together into dialogue with God for purposes of discerning God's current movement in their lives. This kind of sabbatical activity helps to sustain commitments to relational values.

CHAPTER FIVE

Meaning-making in Parsonage Living

The great secret of life is how to survive struggle without
succumbing to it, how to bear struggle without being
defeated by it, how to come out of struggle better than when
we found ourselves in the midst of it.[1]

"The parsonage becomes home for a clergy family for a season. But, it is the congregation's home forever." This view, shared by a clergy spouse is an important starting point for our story-sharing in this chapter. It is important for at least three reasons. First, our own experiences tell us that, while living in a parsonage, there is a sense of residential temporariness while simultaneously striving to create a stable personalized and private dwelling place.

Second, there is tremendous emotion that goes into striving for what is understood by clergy families to be personalized or private abodes. This situation becomes all the more poignant because congregations typically see and give significance to the parsonage in particular ways that conflict with and create distress in clergy families. For example, because the parsonage is the congregation's home, they often perceive it as a public rather than private space. On this basis, the parsonage becomes a "glass house." This unique and often conflicted situation encountered by clergy families may have to do with a kind of an anomaly or modern irregularity related to the loss of village life in the United States. On the one hand, parsonage life may be reckoned as a throwback

113

to village life, where there is a close knit community, where everyone knew everyone else's business, where doors were never locked, and when neighbors came in unannounced and without knocking. On the other hand, church members may tend to want to control parsonage related matters and to know what is going on there as means of ensuring the clergy family's perfect fulfillment of their understanding of the family's role. But, clergy families experience this kind of reality as unsettling and untenable given the honest and necessary need for privacy, especially given the wider church and community ethos within which clergy family life openly occurs.

Third, in the midst of striving, clergy families confront the common human situation of forming meaning. With respect to parsonage living, meaning-making regards approaching "glass house" living in ways that reduce tension and build a worthwhile sense of home along the forward journey of clergy family life despite struggles.

We will keep the opening view in mind as we continue the model of story-sharing undertaken in previous chapters. Here, we will center on parsonage living in our process of telling our stories, unmasking our stories, inviting catharsis, connecting empathically, unpacking our stories, and discerning ways of moving forward. Our purpose for engaging in these practices is to identify previously unseen possibilities in the form of resilient qualities and new approaches needed in forming meaning. That is, our intent is to uncover the kinds of resilience and approaches that help to reduce tension and build a sense of home along the forward journey of clergy family life in the midst of struggles in parsonage living.

The kind of resilience to which we are referring is meant to address head-on clergy families experiences of parsonage life as "glass house living." Indeed, it is critical that attention is given to the private lives of clergy families in this unique circumstance. Clergy families want to know how it is possible to uncover, develop, and maintain resilient practices in the face of very real persistent stories of living "under the microscopic lens and snooper-vision" of church members' eyes, to use the words of a clergy family member. In our focus on resilient practices, we are concerned with how adult clergy family members are able to uncover, develop, and maintain the capacity to be a non-anxious presence and to take a proactive position amidst conflict and tension surrounding church members' expectations of parsonage life and clergy members' views and needs. Proactive resilient practices are called self-differentiation practices where adult family members identify and affirm their own goals and values for living within the parsonage, despite the different pressures and expectations that parishioners might have about how the clergy family might live. To the extent clergy family members carry out these practices, meaning-making proceeds. That is, resilient practices are ways of reducing tension and building a worthwhile sense of home along the forward journey of clergy family life, despite struggles.

It is important to say, too, that identifying and forming the often-unseen potentials and new skills for carrying out resilient practices do not bind meaning-making. Meaning-making also proceeds by discerning God's wind or Spirit at work in our lives through an unfolding plot. We have suggested that it is through the plot revealed in biblical stories or texts that our lives take on significance, despite the difficulties that life presents. It is God's presence in our lives that makes life meaningful by helping us discern God's hope-building activity.

After introducing our own and other cases about family life in the parsonage, we will share additional historical reasons for this leftover artifact from village life. Following this, we will invite you into the story-sharing process.

Our Story

During early years of our ministry, we were a clergy family where Ed was pastor of a small congregation. We regarded the parsonage as our home. On one occasion a seventy-three year old member was walking the streets suffering from a psychotic episode where she believed government agents had taken over her house. She feared going home because she thought they would arrest her, believing that she was receiving social security illegally. This elderly woman was from the southern part of the United States, and her birth records were not accurate. The government had determined that she was eligible for social security benefits, but this was foreign to her. She felt she should not be given anything free. She had worked all her life as a domestic worker, and at some point she had done all the paperwork to secure social security.

Concerned members of our church called us. They did not know what to do, and they told us that she did not have any living relatives. Her husband had died many years earlier, and she also was the recipient of part of his social security benefits. We then set out to find her. We found her, and she thought we were her parents. This was the southern tradition in which she grew up. In the African American community, both clergy and spouse were expected to be the parents of church members. When people did not have relatives, they were expected to turn to the clergy and their families for care. Of course, we realized the expectation. We took her into our home, but her needs were far too great for us to handle. We had to make other arrangements, but this elderly woman never forgave us for failing to keep her in our home.

In a similar manner, a troubling situation arose with a teenage member of the congregation and we were asked to intercede by allowing the teen to stay with us for a period of time. Because of our concern for the teen and desire to help the teen's family, we welcomed the adolescent into the parsonage. However, we were concerned about the precedent that had been clearly set and wondered how far we could or should actually go in our role as a clergy family. In all honesty, looking back, we struggled with feelings of guilt if we refused to respond to the needs of the members. But, we were concerned about the rightful role of the congregation in caring for persons in need, and were able to share this concern at a later time.

The point of these brief references is to highlight that church members have expectations for clergy and their families that can be quite demanding. It also relates specifically to modern anxiety that church members have about life and how it is often focused on the parsonage. Following the next brief vignettes, we will discuss the parsonage and its historical significance that links the clergy family to the modern drama of some congregations to supervise the life of clergy and their families.

Other Clergy Family Vignettes of Parsonage Life

Vignette One

This case study relates to a clergywoman who was moving to a new church appointment. The church was small and because there was no parsonage, they began looking for an affordable rental place for their newly appointed pastor. A longstanding member who had moved to the west coast purchased a house near the church and was planning to move back to the community of his birth. He and his family were killed on the return trip, and seeing the availability of the house, the church acquired it.

The pastor moved into the completely remodeled parsonage. After moving in the pastor said: "Every day, the chair of the trustee board used his keys and came into the house. I was insulted because it looked like he was trying to make sure that my children were not tearing up their property. I felt my family and I had a right to our privacy. About six weeks into the house, I said to the trustee's wife, 'Your husband is not a relative of mine. Why does he have to come into my home everyday?' The wife talked to her husband and he stopped. Our privacy was finally protected. As I think back, I did what I thought was the only way to get the situation taken care of. It should have been the responsibility of the whole church to protect our privacy. But, I'm not sure who I could have talked to or whether going to someone else would have made a difference."

Vignette Two

This story surfaced at a meeting of pastors and their families. The topic focused on tension related to the condition of the parsonage. Many of the families attending the meeting told stories of difficulty conveying to congregations the importance of the parsonage as the private residence in which the clergy family is tenant and the church is landlord.

One pastor voiced his idea that tenants and landlords have particular expectations of each other that are not evident in church and clergy family relations. The pastor said: "For example, the church did not let us inspect the parsonage before we moved in. We were told to just move in. But, on the moving day, we discovered an unkempt place with carpet that was completely worn, frayed, and smelly as the result of pets. We refused to move in until the church did something about the rug and the house in general. Had they allowed us to have an inspection, this problem would have been resolved before our scheduled move-in date."

The pastor went on the say: "It was also a fact that many of the church trustees were unreasonable. The question that kept coming to my mind was whether the church members would want to live in the parsonage. I appealed to the trustee chair in as calm but matter-of-fact manner as I could. The issue actually moved to resolution when the trustee chair talked to other members of the trustee committee on my behalf. He was a gracious man whom all the members respected. He made an analogy between the parsonage situation and the renting of a house. He indicated that if we had rental property, we would fix it so that people would want to rent it. All of a sudden the other trustees understood the problem, and things got fixed. I really give credit to the man who understood it first and was determined to do something about it. I feel good about that." But, the pastor continued, "This problem is what our family has had to endure each time we've moved."

Vignette Three

Many of the pastors and their families felt that they were "between a rock and a hard place" when it came to negotiating parsonage repairs and providing a place in which they felt comfortable enough to invite guests. One pastor was concerned about how the congregation would view him after he had confronted them about the real needs of the parsonage. He said he did not want them to feel he was ungrateful. He did not want this to hinder his efforts to carry out his ministry. At the same time, he did not want his family to be taken for granted and just provided with anything. He had expectations similar to his church members about the quality of their homes; and he wanted the same for his family.

Vignette Four

One pastor owned his own home, which was in driving distance of his new church assignment. He was comfortable with living in his own home, but the church wanted him to live in the parsonage. He finally consented, but also communicated that he would live between both houses. He said that he felt comfortable in his own home because it offered what he and his family needed. "In my own home," he said, "I did not have to depend on the church to do things they did not want to do."

Vignette Five

We were conducting a continuing education event for a seminary in the northeast. In the process of going through the story-sharing stages, a clergywoman presented a problem that involved the parsonage of a congregation in a transitional neighborhood in an inner city. The pastor was leading the congregation and living in the parsonage in a rapidly changing community. All of the members lived outside the community in which the church was situated and continued to voice a great deal of fear and anxiety about the new community surrounding the church. In fact, the members' fear was so strong that they resisted the efforts of the pastor to reach out to the Hispanic community adjoining the church.

The rapid decline of the church membership accompanied the members' relocation to distant residential communities and fears about the changing community around the church. The church was actually in the organizational life cycle trajectory of death; however, the congregation was in the denial stage. The congregation's control over the parsonage became their way of holding onto their historical identity and home in the community even in absentia. Above all, the parsonage and for that matter, the church building, appeared as symbols of the congregation's own space that must be guarded and saved. Even though drug dealers had threatened the pastor's life in the park when she walked the family's dog, the members avowed that there was no need to find another location for a parsonage. Eventually, the pastor and her husband made a personal decision to move to what they felt was a safer community. Their move caused a major uproar within the congregation.

The aforementioned stories point to very real concerns that challenge pastors and their families' positive meaning-making in parsonage living. In the beginning of the chapter, we made the connection between parsonage-related clergy and congregational conflict and the old-time village orientation as well as congregational desires to ensure certain kinds of behavior of pastors and their families. What more may be said about the source of the conflict around parsonage living that appears to erupt in many instances between congregations and clergy families? To answer the question, we will turn briefly to a historical perspective that may shed some light on the dynamics surrounding contemporary parsonage life.

The Historical Cultural Context: A Puritan Leftover

The stories of clergy families tell us that congregations and clergy families have a unique relationship when it comes to parsonage living. It is clear that, in many instances, clergy families experience the parsonage as a place under the control of congregations. This control may be seen as part of a larger framework of congregational sway in the lives of clergy families that has deep roots and motive. And, while this framework does not mitigate the situations of clergy families needing attention, it does provide a basis for reflection and ways of moving forward.

Church historian Brooks Holifield traces the unique circumstance and treatment of clergy families by congregations to the anxiety of laity about contemporary life.[2] He begins his explanation with a citation from Tom Skinner, a noted African American evangelist speaking to a group of ministers. He said Skinner got the attention of the audience by reminding the audience about how some congregations want to control every detail of the pastor's life, even including the attire of the preacher's wife. Skinner talked about a time when congregations authorized and empowered themselves to dictate how ministers and their families should live. For Holifield, the self-authorization by congregations to dictate every detail of the pastors' and their families' lives reflects the anxiety of laity about the uncertainties of life and a desire for a reassuring and authoritative guiding presence. Consequently, the laity's desire for control over the clergy family is meant to ensure that the assigned role the laity gives to this family is upheld.

Holifield's position is that clergy should neither try to escape from nor conform to the expectations and demands. Rather, he says that clergy need to help the laity explore their anxiety and their need for authoritative guidance that underlies their sense of disquiet. This insight is based on Holifield's use of psychodynamic psychological theory. Holifield's use of psychodynamic insight is an attempt to help clergy transcend the expectations placed on them so they can be more effective in ministry. While this is a very helpful suggestion, it is our experience that some clergy tend to disagree. Confronting what is experienced as intimidating, unreasonable, and unrealistic is not easily accomplished. In fact, especially children and spouses of clergy tell of resenting the demands and experience them as an imposition. For clergy and their family members, coming to Holifield's perspective and position could take many years of growing, practice, and reflection.

The point to be made here is that the situation will not likely go away. As a historian especially of the Puritan experience in the colonies, Holifield documents a long historical influence related to the special monitoring of clergy and their families by congregations. Moreover, others recognize the unique situation and treatment of clergy families as cultural givens. Indeed, this has been the conclusion of David and Vera Mace, the founders of the marital enrichment movement.[3] They support the notion that many church members need the pastor and the pastor's family to remain a stable reality in a changing and insecure world and will relate in ways that ensure it.

Carrie Doehring, a pastoral theologian, gives a more contemporary version of the relationship of anxiety and the insecurity of contemporary life. She points out that we live in a culture where attunement or human empathy is sorely lacking given the nature of the break up of relationships. This is often called the collapse of the village. She says that when there is a short supply of relationships in the lives of people, they begin to look toward clergy, parents, work relationships, and other primary relationship for perfect empathy.[4] While other caregivers are not singled out, it is our experience that clergy are quite often the recipients of perfectionist expectations, given the nature of the tradition of expectations that Holifield and the Maces highlight. More specifically, this tradition relates to the desire of the laity for authoritative guidance.

There may be no easy answers to the dilemma of congregational control over parsonage living that many clergy families face. Yet, again, this awareness of the background that underlies a major part of the situation of parsonage living for many clergy families provides a footing for deciding ways of addressing it and finding meaning in parsonage living.

An Invitation to Story-Sharing

As indicated earlier, the story-sharing process will engage you briefly in the story-telling, catharsis, empathic relating, and story unpacking phases. More intensive attention will be given to the final phase of moving forward because of the critical necessity in the meaning-making endeavor of arriving at fitting responses to issues surrounding parsonage living.

We are sure there are many stories that you and your family members can tell about parsonage life. You will have an opportunity to recall an example of dealing with parsonage committees or another experience as a way to explore the kinds of practices you have used to respond to the concerns and pressures related to parsonage living. As you recall your own stories, remember some of the examples that have been told already. If you have had positive experiences, please do not hesitate to tell those stories. In doing so we all might learn some positive practices that have been used from which all of us can learn.

It is important to complete the steps below as part of your family or a small group experience of recall. However, these exercises are best suited for retreat settings where other clergy families are present or with a small group of clergy families with or without a guide. The retreat or other setting utilizing small groups of people will provide the kind of support systems on which to build.

Unmask Your Story

Meaning-making does not happen apart from our own stories and what happens in those stories. As an explicit endeavor or one in which we consciously engage, meaning-making also entails not only our disclosure, but also our interpretation of what has or is occurring in the very real stories of our lives. Telling a story of parsonage living is a way of entering deliberately into the meaning-making endeavor. Create occasions in clergy family units or small groups of clergy families with or without a guide, or in a retreat setting with a guide to explore the nature of parsonage living and ways of making meaning in it. Divide large groups in a retreat setting into small sub-groups or dyads to ensure an opportunity for individual story-sharing and the intimate caring and listening presence of others. Further sharing and reflection in the larger group context may follow small group sharing. The following protocol invites you into the story-sharing and meaning-making endeavor.

Describe the Parsonage Event(s)

- Recall a pleasing event and/or a troubling event that related to parsonage living that involved you, your family, and the congregation and/or parsonage committee.
- What were the events and where did they take place?
- Who were the church members in the events?
- Who were the family members in the event?
- What made the event pleasing? What made the event troubling?

Introduce any Tension or Conflict that Emerged

- What issue(s) surfaced which all had to address?
- Tell as fully as you can what precipitated the tension or conflict or why it happened.
- Describe the relational climate that existed. Was it warm and friendly, or cool and conflicting?
- What were the final results?

SOME CLUES

Our story revealed the congregations' expectation that we assume a parental role for members in difficult situations and open the parsonage for those in need. Although we obliged the congregation by welcoming members in difficult situations in the parsonage, we became aware of our lack of ability to provide sufficient care in one case. With the second situation, we became concerned about the precedent we were setting that could potentially extend beyond our capabilities and our need for privacy. We were also concerned for our usurping the congregation's role in caregiving to needy individuals and families.

Other vignettes of clergy families centered on the ongoing intrusive behavior of church trustees that was settled by the pastor's conversation with the trustee's wife; the poor physical condition of a parsonage, that occasioned the pastor's refusal to move until repairs were made; personal versus church housing, resulting in a dispute following the pastor's decision to live between the two houses; and conflict resulting from the decision of a pastor to move from an unsafe parsonage location to private housing.

Invite Catharsis and Connect Empathically

As you share your stories with your conversation partners, be aware of how you are feeling. If you have negative feelings, please tell them to those with whom you are sharing your story. If you have positive feelings, also share them as well with your conversation partners.

- As you tell your story, get in touch with the feelings you have and put them into words to share as part of your story.
- As you listen, make sure you attend to the story that is being told to you.
- When feelings of others surface, acknowledge them without being judgmental or sharing advice. The key is to help the person share his or her story, and to acknowledge their feelings. This attending helps foster empathic connecting.

SOME CLUES

Even though we felt our own privacy could be in jeopardy if we responded to every situation of need, we nonetheless felt obliged to respond as we did. In the clergy family situation where intrusiveness was the issue, the pastor expressed feelings of indignation because the trustee appeared to be monitoring her family's care of the parsonage. Another expressed feelings of gratitude for a lone church official who understood the magnitude of the issue and acted on behalf of the clergy family. In still another case, the fear and anxiety of the pastor about being in an unsafe parsonage location was matched by the alarm of the congregation about the changing neighborhood and fear of losing the parsonage and church as historic symbols.

Unpack Your Story

When you have told your story, shared your feelings, and feel like you have been heard, take some time to enter into the next phase of the interpretation process with your conversation partner(s). This phase focuses on your getting in touch with the meanings you assign to the event(s) you share about parsonage living. It also entails identifying resilient practices or skills you employed that were helpful in resolving the issues related to parsonage living and dealing with congregations. These forms of resiliency are ones that may be useful in the future. However, it is also important to identify areas of your story where things were not handled as well so that these practices may be avoided in the future. Follow the guides provided below:

- What does it mean that the event(s) you describe happened to you or that you are now experiencing them?
- What did you do or what practices did you follow that helped resolve issues related to parsonage living? Why were the practices helpful?
- What did you do or what practices did you follow that did not help resolve the issues related to parsonage living? Why were the practices of little help?
- Are there any unresolved issues remaining that need to be addressed in the near future? If so, what are they? Share them with your conversation partners if appropriate.
- What now would you say was the outcome of what has already happened? What would you say is the anticipated outcome of what is now happening?

SOME CLUES

Although we were able to explore our concern about the congregation's role in caring for members in trouble, this exploration came after we willingly obliged the congregation's expectations to become caregivers in the parsonage. At that time in our early ministry, we were unable to see ways of negotiating the situation or of identifying alternative approaches. We were concerned about confronting our guilt if we refused to provide care.

The clergywoman in the situation of an intrusive trustee handled the situation with satisfactory outcomes by approaching the trustee's wife. However, this action was not taken until a number of weeks had passed. She wondered if there might have been another way of handling the situation, but it did not seem to come to her at the time, and she was not sure if another approach would have resulted in a positive outcome.

Another clergy was concerned about jeopardizing his ministry, whereas still another pastor who refused to move into an unsatisfactorily maintained parsonage calmly and resolutely appealed to the trustee chairperson who, in turn, was able to remedy the situation.

The Way Forward

Moving forward relates to the continued use of positive practices and skills that you found helpful in resolving past parsonage issues. These positive practices and skills are referred to as resilient practices that might need to be employed as long as you and your family live in parsonages. The practices are pivotal in the meaning-making endeavor. Moving forward also includes identifying those practices and skills you need to develop in order to bring a positive resolution to unresolved issues. This action is important because it forms the basis for interpretive judgment or deciding practical approaches for responding to parsonage living and conflicts and tensions that arise in it.[5] Therefore, central to moving forward is developing needed practices and skills, and then making plans to use them in resolving parsonage concerns in the future. In short, identifying these practices and skills and designing plans for using them are important meaning-making tasks to undertake. Explore the following with your conversation partner(s):

- Review the ways you have handled specific issues related to parsonage living. Identify one or two positive practices or skills you would definitely want to use in the future and tell why.
- What kinds of practices and skills have you heard from other conversation partner(s) that provide some direction for your formation of new practices and skills? Describe what is helpful about them.
- Explore how you intend to develop the practices and skills. Also explore how you will utilize the practices and skills in a current or anticipated unresolved situation.

We will close this chapter by listing some resilient practices that will help you move forward, and we will also provide some clues that disclose key skills. We will do so by returning to the vignette of the pastor who sought out the trustee chairperson to resolve the parsonage issue he and his family confronted. We will also add several new vignettes to illustrate key resilient practices.

Resilient Practices for Meaningful Parsonage Living

The critical questions are: How may pastors find meaning in parsonage situations where they are neither renters nor homeowners? How do they develop the resilient ability to deal with age-old expectations of church members, and still deal with family needs? Finally, how do pastors develop the resilient practice of negotiating parsonage issues while not jeopardizing their ministry in the church?

Answering the questions lies in carrying out the goal of becoming a non-anxious presence in the midst of some very difficult negotiations. A non-anxious presence within the context of parsonage life is the result of the pastor's awareness of his or her own family goals for family life and living, and willingness to take maximum responsibility for his or her own home life and emotional well-being without being reactive or defensive.[6] How pastors move to becoming a non-anxious presence is the heart of meaning-making in parsonage living. For illustrative purposes, let us return to the pastor's vignette.

In the case introduced earlier in this chapter and repeated in part in the section on clues to story-sharing, the clergy demonstrated a capacity for non-anxious presence by approaching the trustee chairperson calmly and resolutely about the parsonage situation. Rather than dealing directly with the committee, the pastor sought to handle it by addressing only one person. The chair had shown empathy with the clergy family's situation. Furthermore, the others on the trustee board respected him. Thus, the pastor perceived openness on the chairperson's part to addressing the parsonage concerns. In addition, the chairperson had no difficulty being open and frank about what he thought, and others listened to him. Therefore, the pastor approached him with the concerns about the parsonage. The pastor's approach resulted in the trustee board's positive response to the chairperson's appeal on behalf of the pastor. Together, the pastor, the chairperson, and the entire board worked out an acceptable solution with which all were satisfied.

The Skill of Being a Non-anxious Presence

The concept of non-anxious presence emerges out of the family therapy tradition, and it is related to the work of family therapist Murray Bowen. Bowen's work made the concept of self-differentiation pivotal.[7] This concept is grounded in the capacity of individuals to become unique separate selves apart from others who make up their family of origin or birth. The capacity for self-differentiation is not individualistic, however. It has two basic tendencies. The first tendency is to become a separate self apart from others. Indeed, this separateness is regarded as basic human nature. The second tendency is the opposite, however. The capacity to become self-differentiated and to achieve increased levels of self-differentiation is accomplished by the individual's remaining in constant contact with her or his family of origin. The capacity for being a non-anxious presence can only be achieved as a result of increased levels of self-differentiation. This capacity is grounded in remaining in constant contact with members of one's own family of origin or birth.

The theory assumes that self-differentiation produces anxiety for the individual attempting to self-differentiate as well as for those within the family of origin. But, as individuals become more self-differentiated, their anxiety lessens. A less anxious and self-differentiated person's behavior is characterized by the capacity to be less reactive, defensive, more proactive, more focused, more self-directed, less externally focused, and less threatened by being different from those in the family of origin.

Family therapists like Murray Bowen and Edwin Freedman believe that the capacity for being a non-anxious presence can be transferred from one's family of origin to other activities, especially leadership in the church or religious institution. In fact, we contend that the capacity for being a non-anxious presence, grounded in the capacity for self-differentiation, is basic for pastors when dealing with the way some congregations relate to clergy families around parsonage concerns. Pastors with low levels of self-differentiation will be more anxious about confrontations with parsonage committees in local churches. The converse is true, however. Those pastors with high levels of self-differentiation will be less anxious and more effective in handling parsonage concerns and issues. In addition, pastors with high self-differentiation also have other positive characteristics, such as, high self-esteem, a heightened sense of personal well-being and feelings of being worthwhile, a healthy attitude toward participation in the lives of others, and a capacity to engage conflicting issues. They also have the capacity to withstand criticism and can remain focused on tasks amidst opposition. In addition, they are able to find ways of affirming themselves despite the disapproval of others.

The above characteristics of being non-anxious and self-differentiated enable pastors to enter into negotiations with parsonage committees. Moreover, these characteristics also influence how pastors relate to their own families of creations—or families pastors form through marriage. High self-differentiation, along with the capacity for being non-anxious, contributes to the self-differentiation of clergy family members. These two capacities promote less anxiety in other family members, and they free up family members to move toward increased levels of self-differentiation. In other words, self-differentiation and being non-anxious presences contribute to the maturing process of members of the clergy family.

Edwin Friedman notes that self-differentiated leaders also contribute to the maturing of church members.[8] Self-differentiated leadership stimulates those in the congregation with high levels of self-differentiation to come forward during times of conflict. The result is that issues can get resolved. Conversely, less self-differentiated leaders get caught up in factionalism, and they find it hard to get issues resolved. Less mature people seem to rule the day.

The point of this lengthy discussion on non-anxious presence and self-differentiation is to promote understanding not only how to resolve parsonage concerns and to provide effective leadership, but also how to enable or foster meaning and hope in glass-house living. Pastors with high self-differentiation are happy with themselves. They feel loved and cared for. They have meaning and purpose in life. They derive pleasure from their relationships and from their work. They have a sense of well-being and assurance, even when things are not going well. They have the capacity for participation in relationships with others as well as with God. They connect regularly with God, and they take periods of Sabbath rest with God where they find spiritual renewal and added energy for continued ministry.

Pastoral self-differentiation and non-anxiousness are derivative of a larger spiritual reality. They are not the source of meaning. The source of meaning is in the person's relationship with God and in continued participation in the faith community. Thus, meaning and hope are spiritual derivatives.

Cultivating Self-Differentiation and Non-Anxious Skills and Practices

Being able to carry out the goal of a non-anxious presence in the face of challenges in parsonage living cannot be automatically assumed. Nor can we take for granted that we are fully self-differentiated. As a result, we may benefit from engaging in steps to assess and cultivate our level of self-differentiation and our ability to be a non-anxious presence. As indicated, one method of becoming a non-anxious presence in the face of challenges in parsonage living is to return to one's family of birth or of origin for the practice it offers us. It is important, then, to begin to plan opportunities to return home in order to practice becoming less anxious. The following plans are grounded in the work of family therapist Murray Bowen.[9] These plans include:

- establishing person-to-person relationships,
- becoming a better observer;
- controlling one's emotional overreactions.

These three practices take time to implement, and Bowen suggests that we use professional family therapists as coaches in order to implement these resilient practices.

The steps recommended above are also consistent with the moving forward phase of the story-sharing process. They assume that the early steps in this process including unmasking the story, inviting catharsis, connecting empathetically, and unpacking the story have already taken place.

Decide to Return Home

- Begin the practices of self-differentiation by making a plan to return home.
- It would be helpful to find a professional or a support group for returning home.
- Plan a time to go home so that you can implement some of the steps of self-differentiation.
- Step 1. Plan to develop a person-to-person relationship with only one family member at a time. It is important to find a place and time when other family members are not around. Moreover, it is important not to take on more than one family member at a time. In fact, to relate to more than one person at a time will undermine your efforts, keep you locked within the family's emotional system, and make it hard for you to differentiate yourself from it. Do the following:
  1. Choose a family member with whom to relate.
  2. Try not to talk about other family members.
  3. Try not to talk about impersonal things.
  4. Rather, find a way to talk about your relationship with this person.
  5. Begin with early relationships in childhood since this is not normally anxiety provoking and would help to build rapport for talking about more anxiety ridden themes later on.
  6. It would be helpful to begin with a parent if he or she is alive and relatively healthy. Otherwise siblings will do. Relatives would be helpful as well if you were close when growing up.

- Step 2. Become an observer and control your emotional reactions. Do the following:
  1. Become an observer. This means observe how family members respond to your efforts to talk about your personal relationships. Sometimes family members might find it hard to talk about your relationship with them. Sometimes they might welcome it. The point is to observe how the person responds.
  2. Control your emotional reactions. Do not attack, counter-attack, confront, or defend yourself. This helps avoid the situation from deteriorating into anger or blaming and assists you

in becoming a better observer. The key is to keep from becoming entangled in the family emotional system and to be self-differentiated.

- Step 3. Report your efforts to your support group or professional coach. Begin to plan the next home visit. You can return to unfinished business with the same person. You might also begin plans for relating to other family members.

Applying Self-Differentiation and Non-Anxious Skills and Practices in the Church

One of the major strategies for handling potentially contentious situations is not to take on the entire committee. A non-anxious strategy is to address the key leader on a one-on-one basis. Recall in the earlier cited vignette that the pastor carried out this strategy in a non-defensive way. The pastor also assumed the legitimacy of the claim that needed to be made to the chairperson of the trustee board. The pastor happened to pick a person who had high self-differentiation, and as a result they were able to see "eye to eye."

In a separate case not presented earlier, an associate pastor consulted with the senior pastor who, in turn, sought further guidance from a denominational official to address costly repairs in the parsonage. This alternative was chosen in advance of going to the parsonage committee, because both the senior pastor and the associate were new to the congregation. The associate approached the senior pastor in a non-anxious way with several alternatives, recognizing the need not to place the pastor in a difficult position with the parsonage committee since he also was new. Prior to presenting the issue to the parsonage committee, however, the senior pastor talked with the district superintendent who understood the associate pastor's concerns and felt they were legitimate. The superintendent urged the senior pastor to advocate on behalf of the associate pastor.

What was helpful in this situation was not just the fact that the senior pastor, the associate pastor, and the superintendent were highly self-differentiated people. The conference also had specific expectations, guidelines, and principles in place for parsonages. The associate pastor was aware of these guidelines and brought them to the awareness of the senior pastor. When the senior pastor and the associate pastor subsequently talked with the parsonage committee, they used the conference parsonage guidelines as the basis for negotiating the changes needed. The problem was resolved with very little conflict.

In this case, as in case one, the associate pastor demonstrated the capacity for being a non-anxious presence. The pastor completed necessary homework by researching the conference guidelines that provided an objective basis for presenting the case. The pastor approached the senior pastor who was highly self-differentiated and showed empathy toward him by not wanting to put him in a difficult situation. All of these personal dimensions demonstrated a high level of self-differentiation and non-anxious skill.

In a final case, a pastor owned his own home. He was appointed to a church eighty miles away from his home. His new congregation wanted him to live in the parsonage. Because this would be his family's first time living in a parsonage, and because he was accustomed to being his own landlord, he had some concerns that he felt were legitimate. He knew it was important to get off on the right foot in the new church, so he began a strategy to get his questions answered about the parsonage prior to moving.

First, he asked the superintendent to take him to the new parsonage during daylight hours. He particularly wanted to see the neighborhood because of his concerns for an acceptable environment for his wife and children. He learned that the church was not next door to the church, which he considered a real plus. He and his wife discussed the need to maintain some privacy, and discovering that the church had built the parsonage away from the church made him feel good in preparing to enter the congregation.

Several members from the parsonage committee joined him and the district superintendent at the parsonage, and he was able to ask more questions. He said they responded very positively, and he felt that these people had empathy for parsonage families. He did see some things that needed attention. The parsonage committee indicated that it would take a few months to develop plans to meet the needs he expressed. The pastor felt that this was a good thing and supported the development of the plans. The pastor was particularly encouraged by the committee's view of the parsonage as an investment in the ministry of the church, and that it was important to the congregation to ensure the satisfaction of the pastor and his family. The committee also saw their care for the parsonage as a way to free the pastor to do ministry. The pastor expressed gratitude for the committee members' maturity and understanding of the importance of making his family comfortable so he could do ministry.

Another plus was the fact that the parsonage committee was full of self-differentiated people. They saw themselves as partners in ministry with the pastor. Therefore, they wanted to be team players within reason. The pastor had no difficulty with this since he also had high self-differentiation. He also knew that he would be accountable as well as hold them accountable in the partnership. Because of this initial visit to the parsonage with the district superintendent and with members of the parsonage committee, he and his family were excited about embarking on the new adventure of parsonage living. Beyond this, he was also excited about starting his ministry with this church since he perceived them as eager to be in ministry.

A Final Word on Moving Forward

The story-sharing process ends with a moving forward phase. Brief additional comments on that phase will be made here. First, it is important in this phase for clergy families to gain forthright awareness of the reality of non-changeable and non-negotiable dimensions of being clergy families. Moving forward also involves the recognition of changeable and negotiable dimensions of parsonage living. And, moving forward involves discerning how God is involved in our process of moving forward, and finding ways to cooperate with where God is moving us. Finally, it involves engaging in story-editing as we examine our beliefs and convictions related to what it means to be members of clergy families. Story-editing involves envisaging the options and opportunities for changed behavior and thinking brought about by cooperating with what God is doing to move us forward. Moving forward, then, is about responding to the winds of promise with recognition that these winds foster hope and resilience in our lives as clergy families.

In moving forward, the assumption is that the clergyperson in clergy families is most especially proactive in getting in touch with key parsonage-related issues affecting his or her existence and the needs of family members. In this chapter, we have dealt with the parsonage phenomenon and how the parsonage has become the battleground for the control of the life of the pastor and the pastor's family. The effort of church members to control the lives of clergy families has been linked dominantly to contemporary anxieties that parishioners have about life, and how they seek stability in their lives. The parsonage becomes the stage on which the drama of control is often acted out.

This chapter revealed that there are at least two major conversations about parsonage life taking place in which clergy families are engaged. These conversations include the Puritan legacy of congregations controlling the lives of clergy families, and the expectation that leaders in clergy families become self-differentiated persons who have developed the capacity to practice being non-anxious presences in the face of parsonage pressures from the congregations. The way forward, then, is for the leaders in clergy families, and especially the clergyperson, to increase their capacity for being a non-anxious presence through the practice of increasing self-differentiation.

CHAPTER SIX

Managing Catastrophic Events and Other Devastating Circumstances

Often times of crisis are times of discovery, periods when we cannot maintain our old ways of doing things and enter into a steep learning curve. Sometimes it takes a crisis to initiate growth.[1]

When we began writing this book, hurricanes Katrina and Rita had not occurred. However, during the completion stage, these two catastrophic events struck New Orleans and the Gulf Coast. Clergy families were among the many whose lives were turned upside down in the wake of the devastation. As the stories of clergy families who survived the hurricanes began to unfold, we were reminded that, as clergy families, we are not immune to the ravages and trauma of unforeseen events and the difficult task of managing our lives in their aftermath. We are not beyond the need for care and succor. Out of this recognition, we have included this chapter to invite specific story-sharing focused on ways to manage tragedies that befall us along our journeys as clergy families.

Many stories have been told and retold in this work, and some may already be regarded as heartrending. Throughout each chapter, we have shared our stories, the stories of others, and a story-sharing process. We have invited clergy family members to tell and reflect on personal stories in order to discover the presence of facilitating and sustaining resilience. We have maintained that telling and retelling stories together in individual family settings, in small groups of clergy families during organized retreats and other times, or in special forms of sabbatical rest build bridges for self-discovery and growth. Indeed, the stories we have lived or are now experiencing and tell "educate the self and others including the young."[2]

This orientation to story-sharing will continue in this chapter. However, here our attention turns expressly to stories of catastrophic events and other devastating circumstances as well as to resilient practices needed to manage these tough situations and tend to self-care. Our movement toward the story-sharing process will be framed by an understanding of the nature of catastrophic events and devastating circumstances, unique challenges clergy families face in addressing these difficult experiences, and the connection between managing events and the practice of resilience.

A Framework for Recalling Stories of Catastrophic Events and Devastating Circumstances

This chapter emphasizes two types of stories. The first story type focuses on experiences of tremendous loss and anguish due to public disasters. Public disasters are catastrophic events such as hurricanes, tornadoes, floods, and other natural calamities sometimes called "acts of God" as well as accidental or deliberate human deeds such as infernos, acts of terror, and war. These events typically result in large scale human suffering and major loss or damage to persons and possessions.[3] The second type of story discloses anguish and grief brought on by devastating events such as unexpected, sudden or terminal illness of self or loved ones, the death of loved ones, or disablement due to accidents or human negligence. As a consequence of either catastrophic or devastating events, individuals may experience deep anguish, long-lasting emotional trauma, memory flashbacks, and sometimes chronic preoccupation with their particular experience or happening.

Challenges to Addressing the Stories

Clergy families experience what some call "the wilderness" of responding to catastrophic events and other devastating circumstances by virtue of the fact that these extreme difficulties of life happen to us just as they happen to others. But, there are unique challenges to addressing these situations because of the role of clergy and often clergy family members as community leaders, parent figures, caregivers and witnesses to ultimate meaning.[4] These challenges must not be overlooked. Particularly in the case of public disasters, church members tend to view especially the pastor as God's representative. Due to this role assignment, in the throes of disaster, members may consider the pastor as having protective power that has either failed or needs to be available in spite of the clergy and clergy family's own circumstance of suffering and loss. In an attempt to respond to church members, clergy may not tend fully to the self's or the family's needs.[5]

In the case of both public disasters and other devastating circumstances, clergy family life unfolds in view of congregations and the larger public. As a result, there may be some reluctance on the part of clergy families to enter into lament while in the throes of loss, or to struggle with questions of faith for fear of modeling blasphemous behavior. Indeed, we may label ourselves guilty of denying the very faith we espouse. "After all," we query, "aren't we supposed to be 'perfect' models of the practice of faith?" Yet, in all truthfulness, in order for the process of managing or coping with catastrophic events to move toward a hope-filled perspective and hope-directed action, honest lament and questions of faith must emerge. Indeed, a part of this honesty is accepting that lament is not blasphemy or denying God's existence. Rather, lament is complaint to God with the expectation of God to respond.

Moving through and beyond the lament also happens when we link our lives with the unfolding story of God revealed in scripture and in faith communities. We will also be reminded later in this chapter that lament is part of the biblical story. Lament is a biblical process that enables us to experience God's presence amidst pain and leads us beyond pain to praise. Our invitation in this chapter is for new or renewed discovery of this aspect of the Christian faith. Moreover, the story-telling we invite in this chapter is not simply to link with scripture in helpful ways, but with caring others who open the way for our discovery or recovery of lives of meaning, hope, and significance. Through insight from scripture and the self's gift of caring others, we become aware of the winds of promise.

Managing Events as a Form of Resilient Practice

The questions may well be asked: What does managing catastrophic events and other devastating circumstances mean? How may we manage the pain of traumatic events amidst public scrutiny and expectations? What images, metaphors, or faith stories help us move through raging storms of tragedy to the winds of promise?

The term, "manage" is a vital action word that refers to our ability to cope with and survive the stormy blast of difficult circumstances and events that threaten our well-being or our will to continue on in life with purpose, meaning, and hope. The term points to our ability to cope with and survive life-bending winds of pain by seeing and grasping the human and spiritual lifelines or opportunities that move us to the next step, and the next, and the next. To this extent, managing or coping with tragedy becomes a problem-solving and faith-constructing, or faith-embracing, process. And, this process necessarily includes telling the story or translating our experiences into words for its cathartic effect and resources that can become building blocks for the journey ahead.[6]

With regard to story-sharing, Gerard Egan reminds us that it is typically easier "to talk about problem situations than about unused opportunities. However, the flip side of just about every problem is an opportunity."[7] This is not to say that the process of managing must in some way deny the presence of pain or struggle. The real stories of catastrophe and the feelings that attend the telling must come forth. But, it is essential that we struggle with hidden or unused resilient practices and opportunities found in a faith perspective and in answering questions such as those posed by Egan:

- What are my unused skills/resources?
- Which of these am I failing to use?
- What opportunities do I let go by?
- What ambitions remain unfulfilled?
- What could I be doing that I'm not doing?
- Which role models could I be emulating?[8]

In what follows, we will present a story of a clergy family who survived the catastrophe of hurricanes Katrina and Rita as well as clergy family vignettes of other devastating circumstances including our own. We will then move to the process of story-sharing.

Survival in the Wake of Katrina and Rita

A retreat for close to a hundred clergy family members became a place for these persons to tell their stories of surviving the ravages of hurricanes

Katrina and Rita. The families shared first in small caring groups, but were also invited to do so in the large group setting according to their need and comfort level. A small group encouraged one woman to tell her story to the entire group. She agreed to share it and was joined briefly by her clergy husband in story-sharing the day after her husband showed pictures of the irreparable damage to the home they had owned for thirty-five years. The essence of the story is as follows:

She said that she and her husband had two small churches in New Orleans. The height and force of the water damaged their home to the extent that it could not be salvaged. Both she and her husband told of losing not only their home, but also treasured memorabilia and numerous items of personal value, reflecting years of marriage and family life. Their words were: "We were not able to take anything we cherished other than our lives."

The clergy spouse then began to express with deep anguished feelings about how one of the congregations responded. She said, "They were really hostile. One member called us in Houston, where we had to relocate, and accused me of taking their pastor away from them. I was so hurt that they were not concerned about our losing our home and having no place to live or that my husband had lost his income. We were actually forced to move to Houston where many of the employees from my workplace were sent, because the company had to evacuate New Orleans. Our members did not understand that there was no way and nowhere for us to return. We lost our home. There was nowhere to live, and there was no way of earning a living." Tears welled up in her as she told the group about her experience of surprising and unreasonable members' expectations of her and her husband. She continued, "They need to understand that my husband and I were just as devastated as they were. Our lives were disrupted and we lost everything too. How could they expect us to come back when we had no place to live or any income other than mine?" She then became quite still.

After a brief period of silence, she began to cry. She recalled the year preceding the hurricane, and all of a sudden her lament shifted in an unexpected direction. She said that the retreat was the kind of Sabbath rest that she needed to put things in perspective. She then began to share an experience that occurred approximately one year ago, when she was one hundred and fifteen pounds heavier than she was at present. She was in the hospital with the expectation of imminent death. In her terminal state, hooked up to life support systems, her family was told to come pay their last respects and say their goodbyes. She then told of the point when the life supports were removed. "But, instead of dying," she said, "my vital signs began to stabilize. I asked and they agreed to send me home the very next day."

She continued, "Over the last few weeks, I have not had time to really see what God has done in my life. It is clear to me now. The goodness of God a year ago when God brought me out of a death situation has allowed me to talk again about God's goodness in bringing us through the hurricanes." She then drew attention to the tarnished and mold-covered cross she had retrieved from the remains of her home. She had placed the cross on the altar during the opening moments of the retreat. "This cross," she said, "is a symbol of God's continued faithfulness. The real point isn't that we lost everything or even that our members are angry with us. The real point is that we made it through the storm. God's faithfulness gives me reason to have faith to go on." She also exclaimed, "I am not going to clean the mold and the tarnish from the cross, because I want to remember how faithful God is in the moments when life seems so bleak. The cross is a sign that we are not victims. We are survivors."

In bringing her story-telling to conclusion, she began to talk about the way forward. She concluded that God spared her life the previous year so that she could tell others about God's saving grace and power when things appear to be at their worst. She passionately conveyed that just as the doctor's prognosis of her imminent death was not the end of the story, neither hurricane Katrina nor Rita are the last word. She told of a vision of her ministry for the future as that of encouraging those who were victims of Katrina and Rita to become survivors rather than victims. She identified herself as a survivor and not a victim, and declared that her life was spared so she can teach others how to be survivors.

Personal and Other Vignettes of Devastating Circumstances

We had heard that the loss of a child is among the most devastating experiences a parent can have. But, the reality of this pronouncement did not really sink in until our daughter, Diana Kay, died two days after birth. There were no words to describe the grief and anguish. There was only what Anne described as a deep, dark, and lonely pit from which there seemed no air and no escape. The task of ministry seemed to continue for Ed until one day during preparation for the Sunday sermon, the weight of the loss brought his own tears and wailing. We held each other but, still, the grief was overwhelming and our birth families lived far away from where we were in ministry. Our church members tried as best they could to be consoling, but it was clear that they did not—could not—fully comprehend what we were going through. The statement from several, "At least you did not get to know her well," was hurtful. It deepened Anne's experience of a hole of isolation and, for a period of time, her desire not to relate to the members. The loss was so devastating that she still does not remember Diana Kay's graveside service and burial.

A move across state lines beyond where Diana Kay was buried compounded the sense of loss for Anne and her reluctance to relocate out of guilt for abandoning our child or leaving her in a distant grave. However, Anne was able to manage this new sense of devastation because she unburdened the difficulty during a stopover at the home of Ed's parents on the way to the new location. Ed's Dad responded to the anguished story of leaving the place of Diana Kay's grave by recounting the story of the creation of humankind from the dust of the earth and the return of the same to the earth upon death. His concluding words were, "So, since Diana Kay has returned to the earth and is now part of the earth, there is nowhere on earth you can go where she is not." The way forward began at this point.

After moving, Anne had a series of three dreams that continued the forward motion into the winds of promise. In Anne's words, "In the first dream, I was in the pit of smothering darkness. But suddenly, in the midst of the darkness, an illumined hand appeared and a voice spoke saying, 'This is the hand of God that will lead you.' I awakened with a feeling of serenity. The second dream came later and revealed Diana Kay in the heavenly home. She was the age she would have been at the time of the dream. She was beautiful, radiant and best of all, happy. I awakened with a sense of release. In the third dream sometime later, I heard only a voice speaking in what appeared as an open airy space where I breathed with great ease. In the midst of that space, a voice spoke, 'Take heart! You shall have many more children than you could ever have biologically.' I awakened with hope. For me, God's hope for us as a family was made clear in those dreams. Looking back on it now, God created the future into which I resolutely walked to discover the richness and truth of that final dream."

In an earlier chapter, we mentioned briefly Ed's heart surgery. Our account tells of its devastating nature. This event came after a lengthy period of Ed's experiencing chest pains. Over time, the medications prescribed for conditions unrelated to the heart failed to quell his increasing chest discomfort. Finally after difficulty in moving only a few steps without difficulty, he was sent for further tests and finally entered the hospital for an outpatient procedure, called a heart catheterization. Immediate open heart surgery began upon the discovery of a nearly closed main artery.

"Shortly after the seven hour surgery had begun," Anne recalls, "a nurse came to me and said in a matter-of-fact manner I have never forgotten, 'Your husband was rushed into surgery with a coronary occlusion that is often a 'widow-maker'. The situation is critical. You may pick up his clothes and wait in the surgical unit waiting room.'" Yet, later, Ed recalled that in the split second before the anesthesia took hold, he shouted to God, "I'm not ready to die!" He actually became what the doctor described as a miracle man. He lived! He also remembered that during the time of recovery in the hospital, God spoke back to him and said, "Do you accept what I am doing in your life?" Ed's response was, "I do." He described this answer as his avowal to address straightforwardly issues of intimacy as well as to continue his ministry forthrightly.

At the time of this period of anguish, we were caring for Ed's parents whom we had welcomed into our home after his mother's diagnosis of Alzheimer's disease. On the same day as Ed's surgery, one of Anne's brothers also underwent open-heart surgery. Then, shortly after, Ed's only brother was diagnosed with terminal cancer and another brother of Anne underwent a kidney transplant. Anne recalls, "These were tough times with deep questions about how we would be able to withstand the onslaught of so much. I confess to crying out, 'God, where are you? What are you doing?' Praying, however feebly, became the by-word; and giving thanks for just being able to wake up each morning," as my forbears would say, 'in my right mind and able to put my feet on solid ground and walk ahead marked the daily sojourn.' A blessing came in the form of a very close friend who took an extended period off from work and came from another state to be with and care for us. I was reminded that God does work in mysterious and unexpected ways."

Although Ed survived, there are other clergy families whom we know or have heard about whose experiences of their loved ones' devastating terminal illness or sudden death created a brutally hard and long road to renewed hope. In one case, the widow of a clergy who died from a terminal illness told of her bitterness at God for "snatching her husband from her." In another situation, the incapacitating stroke of a pastor's spouse brought wrenching difficulty in providing care, continuing pastoral responsibilities, and raising the family's children. In these circumstances, persons question why and tell of an honest surge of anger that lingers awhile. But, they also confess that, most often with help from caring others within and beyond their congregations, they were able to come to grips with reality and feel the breath of God that gave them renewed strength for what some called "the journey through the wilderness." One person said, however, "Often I just felt alone with no one to call out to. But, somehow, I was able to pass beyond the midnight hour when the first ray of the new day's dawning reminded me that 'weeping endures for the night, but joy comes in the morning.'"

An Invitation to Story-Sharing

We now invite you into the story-sharing process. However, we want to suggest that clergy and family members enter this process in the presence of a skilled helper. Whether in a retreat setting, in small clergy family clusters, or in individual family contexts, guidance of a skilled helper is warranted because of the emotion evoked by recalling present and past experiences of catastrophic events and other devastating circumstances.

The retreat for clergy family survivors of hurricanes Katrina and Rita is an example of guided story-sharing. In the presence of retreat planners and skilled helpers, including pastoral caregivers and a medical doctor, this retreat created time for persons to tell and retell the stories of what had happened to them. The planners and helpers knew that persons must tell and retell their stories because doing so and connecting with biblical stories allows immobilizing emotions to surface as well as personal and spiritual resources to emerge that are needed to manage the journey ahead. The task of the helpers was also to be the kind of attending presence, listener, prompter, and encourager that formed an environment of openness, trust, and willingness of clergy family members to share their stories.

Because the concern here is with both catastrophic events and other devastating circumstances, it is important to remember that the two situations are different. It is helpful to talk about the difference between the two. Moreover, it is necessary to recognize that, although the emotional responses may be similar to both kinds of stories, the source of those responses and the way the sources are talked about will differ. Likewise, emotional responses will vary from person to person. Sensitivity to these variations is essential and is demonstrated through encouraging persons to come from their own vantage point without judging their point of departure and unfolding story. With this is mind, the following process is provided for use in intentionally planned times for clergy family story-sharing with the skilled helper(s).

Unmask Your Story

The following protocol is designed to assist clergy family members in engaging in story-sharing focused on catastrophic events and other devastating circumstances.

Describe a Catastrophic Event or Other Devastating Circumstance

- Recall a time when you or your family faced a catastrophic event or a devastating circumstance. Remember that catastrophic events are public disasters such as hurricanes, tornadoes, floods, and other natural calamities as well as accidental or deliberate acts of humans causing widespread destruction such as fires, acts of terror, and war. Other devastating events are unexpected, sudden or terminal illness of self or loved one, the death of loved ones, or disablement due to accidents or human negligence. Remember also that it is not unusual for these events to be accompanied by deep anguish, long-lasting emotional scars, memory flashbacks, and sometimes chronic preoccupation with the experience. As a result, the depth of feeling associated with the experience will emerge and rightfully so in the process of story-sharing.
- What took place and who were present?
- What were the circumstances surrounding the event?

Introduce the Tension or Conflict

- Talk about the issues and concerns that confronted you and your family in this event.

- What issues were difficult to resolve?
- How have these issues and concerns affected your family members?
- What issues still remain today?

After talking about the tension or conflict, recall the role of the congregation in the event. Pay particular attention to the expectations they had toward you and your family. Try responding to the following:

- What were the expectations of church members toward you during your period of facing loss?
- Describe a specific event in which the expectations of church members became apparent.

SOME CLUES

The clergy spouse who told her story of surviving the hurricanes highlighted the conflict that arose between her and the church members because of the members' expression of anger resulting from perceptions of the pastor's abandonment of them. It is helpful to add here that, at the retreat for survivors of hurricanes Katrina and Rita, the families' stories varied, especially with regard to the impact of the events on their relationship with and responses of church members. For example, one pastor indicated that the expectations of his members intensified in the face of Katrina, and they expected him to be present. He told of his awareness that clergy and their families represent Presence, and he emphasized the capital *P*. Another pastor indicated that there were no unusual expectations communicated by his congregation. In fact, he told of their expression of appreciation for his caring and tending to them and their desire to know what was happening to his family in order to provide needed help.

In Anne's story, tension arose from what, for her, were uncaring comments by church members following our child's death. Unknowingly, the members attempt to be helpful brought pain and Anne's retreat into isolation. A later move beyond the geographic region of burial prompted a new kind of conflict.

Invite Catharsis and Relate Empathically

Especially with regard to catastrophic events and devastating circumstances, in order for story-sharing to be cathartic, it is necessary to be aware of some cautions. As with anyone else, catastrophic events and devastating circumstances strongly impact the lives of clergy families. This impact can be so great that family members may be reluctant to enter fully into the story-sharing process because it promises to be simply too intense. Some family members may not want to risk sharing out of the need to be protective of thoughts, feelings, or treatment of them by others. They might not want to expose before others and to the self what they perceive as their failure in handling or averting a particular situation of loss, anguish and grief, or their perceived inadequacy in moving forward.[9]

Even though family members need and want catharsis, they may need intentioned, special support. This support may be given in the form of the guide's and others being fully present with them and being attentive to what they say and don't say orally, or through body language, without any value judgment attached to it. Prompting questions such as the ones given above and below may help family members begin to put words to what they experienced, what they did during and after the experience, and how they felt about it. But, they may need support in the form of the listeners' being wholly present and fully attuned to what persons are saying about the nature of their experience, what they did, and how they felt.[10] With these cautions in mind, follow the earlier questions with the following ones focused directly on affect and responses to it:

- What feelings surface now as you recall the event shared above?
- What are your feelings about the congregation's attitudes, treatment, or expectations of you during and after the event?
- What changes have evolved in your feelings? What have you done to resolve difficult feelings or to appreciate positive feelings?
- What does each family member have to say in response to the aforementioned questions? (Responses from family members, including children, is key. Encourage not only oral sharing, but also drawing, music, dramatization, or dance, which may be followed by oral sharing.)

Some Clues

At the retreat for clergy families who were survivors of hurricanes Katrina and Rita, we made sure each person was part of a small group and remained in the same small group throughout the duration of the weekend retreat. Members of each group were invited to share in the large group context only if they felt comfortable doing so. As indicated earlier, a pastor's spouse agreed to tell her story to the entire group because of the encouragement and support of her small group. In sharing, she told amidst tears of her lament and chagrin at the attitudes of the church members. But, she became very still and was affirmed in her need to remain in her moments of silence. No one intruded on those moments or asked any questions. She was simply allowed "to be."

Unpack Your Story

Unpacking stories makes possible clergy family members' attempts to uncover a "fuller picture" and to grasp what has already been done or needs to be done to move beyond catastrophic events and devastating circumstances. In this way, the practice of unpacking lends itself to identifying resilient practices and resources already used, ones that remain unrecognized, partially used or unused, and next steps. It is an attempt to explore both positive and negative story aspects. Importantly, facilitating the unpacking practice requires an ongoing presence of empathic relating on the part of the guide(s) and others who are present. Explore the following:

- Return to your story.
- Share one or two dimensions of your story that has generated or is now bringing up the most energy or emotion. What more can you say about where that energy or emotion was and/or is coming from?
- Say something about any issues or feelings that are not yet resolved.
- Say something about what you did or are now doing to alleviate your deep hurt or feelings about what has happened to you. What has been helpful? What has not been helpful?
- In what ways have others been a help to you and/or your family? Who would you name as helper(s) or guide(s) on whom you could call along the way? What is the nature of the help they could give?

Some Clues

In the earlier story of the pastor's wife who survived the hurricanes, much energy was around the church members' attitude and her lamenting the loss of everything. As in the psalms of lament, there was a sudden reversal in her speech and demeanor. At one point, she shifted scenes in her story from the difficult period in the aftermath of the catastrophe to an experience of grave illness a year earlier. Her focus changed to her reckoning with her faith whereupon she linked faith then with faith now. Her faith became a key resource. What she appreciated the most and what helped her to shift from lament to praise was not only remembering the goodness of God in restoring her life a year ago, but also God's faithfulness in bringing them out alive from the hurricanes.

Amidst Ed's emergency open heart surgery and the compounding distress caused by other devastating family crises, Anne confessed to raising deep questions about how we were going to be able to manage the situation. She called it "tough times" in which feeble attempts to pray gave way to giving thanks for simple things like waking up and walking ahead. In this story, help came in the form of a revered proverbial saying of forbears and from a close friend. In our story of moving after the death and burial of our daughter, Ed's dad became an influential helper. The resources Anne identified were both inner and outer. In the clergy family vignettes following our story, persons also identified inner as well as outer resources found within and beyond the congregation. It was clear from our own and other stories that the ability to express grief through crying was evident. This way of expressing deep feelings appeared as normal. Persons admitted struggling with anger and bitterness at God before coming to a place of feeling and acknowledging a renewal of strength.

The Way Forward

Moving forward is about identifying the plot that was at work in the stories of catastrophic events and other devastating circumstances. A plot emerges as we explore images, symbols, metaphors, and pictures that emerge as our stories are told. The time of unpacking the story set the stage for moving forward. By identifying images, symbols, and pictures, we get a glimpse of the unfolding plot, including God's involvement in it and new or renewed awareness of our wherewithal to continue on life's journey with hope. Refer to the following guide to assist the practice of envisioning that journey:

- What images, symbols, metaphors, or pictures in your story offer you a promising way of seeing your way forward?

- Describe the images, symbols, metaphors, or pictures. What meaning(s) do they hold for you, and how may they empower you to move forward?
- Where is God at work in your unfolding future?
- What possibilities do you see for your future? What ways do you see yourself moving forward? Given the possibilities, what key one(s) would you choose and what will you do to make it come alive?
- Be as specific as you can about the steps you need to take in order to move forward.

SOME CLUES

The pastor's wife who survived the hurricanes lifted up the tarnished and molded cross retrieved from the ruins of her home as a symbol of God's presence. For her, this encrusted cross held such powerful meaning for moving forward as survivors rather than victims, that when life seemed bleak, she refused to clean it. She came to the realization that God spared her from dreadful illness and a catastrophic storm for the purpose of sharing her story and teaching others how to be survivors. She envisioned her way forward in a ministry capacity.

In Anne's story, the reenactment of the creation narrative by her father-in-law facilitated her process of relocation. Her way of working through horrendous events and circumstances included praying, though feebly, and the metaphor of being able to continue "in my right mind." She also cried out to God and discovered later God's presence through the presence of a friend that made possible her ability to persevere. Ed recalled that, at the brink of emergency surgery and after, he entered into conversation with God and answered affirmatively God's question to him, "Do you accept what I am doing in your life?" In other instances, the story-tellers used the image of "the journey through the wilderness," to describe their circumstances, and one lifted up the scriptural picture of "weeping endures for the night, but joy comes in the morning."

These images, symbols, metaphors, and pictures in the stories became not simply ways of describing what had been happening in persons' lives, but methods for their embracing a sense of purpose and direction for the road ahead. The images, symbols, metaphors, and pictures became means of empowering persons to move beyond catastrophic and devastating life events into the winds of promise.

Concluding Words

The retreat for clergy families who survived hurricanes Katrina and Rita concluded with two significant and creative rituals that helped the families remember our faith story and to physically act out the story. We formed a circle. We turned to our right and placed our hands on the shoulders of the one in front of us. With our hands on the shoulders of the person in front of us, we took two steps forward and one back symbolizing the journey and pilgrimage of the Christian life. This movement reminded us that the Christian plot is a hopeful one, but there are many setbacks. But, while there are setbacks, the direction of the Christian plot is always moving forward toward the ends that God intends, and we do embrace and act on this plot by marching in step in support of one another. Partaking of Holy Communion followed this communal ritual. The closing words of the retreat organizers were, "What a fitting end to our time of Sabbath, of putting our lives in divine perspective and remembering God's faithfulness to us, despite tragedies that befall us."

While engaging the stories that come forth in this chapter and the preceding ones, a variety of painful memories may surface. You may also become aware of unresolved issues. These memories and issues may call for further attention. You should not be embarrassed or feel that you are alone when you discover the need for further professional help to explore the concerns and issues in greater depth.

EPILOGUE

The Journey Forward: A Matter of Time

Time [is]. . . an attribute of relationships, rather than a "thing" to be exchanged or spent by individuals. Scarcity of time, in that perspective, becomes scarcity of access to relationships.[1]

When pastors embark upon the journey of ministry, family members automatically join the sojourn. There is no question that the forward journey takes us into places we could never have imagined, with people who have filled our lives with joy, laughter, challenge and the realness of everyday existence. There also is no question that the realities of parish life for clergy families demand special attention along the way and times of Sabbath.

The kind of Sabbath into which we have invited families throughout the preceding pages is time together for story-sharing, spiritual renewal, and sustenance—time for honing in on inner strengths and outer resources, and ways to put them to work. We have called this process "building and maintaining resilience" in order to face into winds of promise. However, because it is so easy today to become enmeshed in a frantic pace of what is presumed to be immediate necessities of the ministry calling, clergy may be prone to say, "Time is our worst enemy!"

In the prologue, we alluded to the reality that all of us are part of a fast-paced, technological, productivity, and material-driven social milieu that foments a problematic conception of time. There is a sense in which "time consciousness and time economy are ever-present guides to human behavior . . . despite our having an abundance of so-called 'time-saving devices.'"[2] Family time is at a premium. Full schedules contribute to a constant sense of rushing. Competing priorities result in decisions that cancel out the very kinds of experiences that can take us beyond the stormy gales of life into winds of promise.

In all honesty, clergy are not alone in this dilemma. John Gillis sites research that shows "laments about the lack of family time have become so common that they go unquestioned and unanalyzed. Not only are we told that family members spend less time together, but the quality of that which counts today as family time—dinners, holidays, vacations—had diminished."[3] Gillis meticulously reviews historical patterns of family time that affirm similar issues across the centuries. However, what is new seems to be what he calls "the nature of contemporary ritual and quality time themselves."[4] There is a problem with the frenetic quality of time caused by speeding up activities and "clumping" numerous activities together in a single span of time. We want to hurry up and finish what we're doing so we can go on to the next thing. During meal times and times of celebration, such as at Thanksgiving, dinnertime includes a conglomeration of communal and separate activities such as eating, watching football, computer games, newspaper reading, and conversation. There is also the tendency on the part of parents to saturate children's time with activities deemed necessary to enhance their life chances—an inclination that has resulted in the term, "the hurried child."[5]

The current dilemma brings us back to our reference in the prologue to Gertrud Mueller Nelson's poignant question: "Have we packed our lives with such a frantic pace in search of elusive happiness that God cannot get a word in edgewise?"[6] The struggle today for both clergy and clergy family members, as for others, is to slow down and "de-clump" our activities. We cannot presume that the answer to how to do it will come in the form of an earth-shaking revelation or in a seemingly blazing or fierce "Aha." Rather, the answer may simply come as it did for Elijah—neither in the earthquake or the fire, but rather in the quiet wind through which the words of God emerged: "Elijah, what are you doing here?" Today, that question invites clergy to consider: What are we doing here in our families?"

Importantly, responding to the question leads us to the matter of values—the conception of what is of utmost importance or what we most desire that will give us structure, purpose, and meaning. Kim McGarraugh Jones reminds us that we make choices on the basis of this conception. The way we use time is shaped by our values.[7] But, more than this, our view of the nature and use of time becomes part of our value orientation. Thus, if family and family time are cherished values, then we must be guided by this conception. We must act on it! How do we do it? We want to suggest that clergy along with clergy family members and ecclesial heads may need to re-conceptualize time and create or re-create the steps needed to ensure a promising relational journey or what Jon Hendricks calls "generative futures" for clergy families.[8]

Re-conceptualizing Time

The first step in the re-conceptualization of time is to admit that the concept of time in fast-paced, technologized, commodified society often functions as an obstacle to purposeful and meaningful clergy family time. As part of this acknowledgement, we consider the limitations of the commodified values inherent in the proverbial sayings: "Time must not be wasted." "Time must be conserved." "Time must be spent wisely." And, we move toward a view of *creating time.* This notion of creating time centers on the formation of moments to be and become related to one another significantly. In this view, time is not a commodity to be utilized or viewed in economic terms. Rather, time is created for the sake of and in the service of family wholeness. When lived with intentionality, created time becomes *relational time* and *sacred time.*[9]

Relational Time

Relational time refers to the experience of family members' intentional and deeply felt receptive and responsive presence with one another. *Priority*—making wise choices that center on building and nurturing relationships—guides the expression of relational time. Moreover, a quality of *relational time* is that of *being present* with one another in language conversationally. When families enter into *relational time*, they "carry out the important function of communicating and interacting with one another," to use the words of Kim McGarraugh Jones.[19] In this regard, Jones reminds us that time together in some families may not be positive and may evoke or aggravate conflict. But, she adds that in this regard, the question may be raised: "If the practice of examining values and incorporating quality family time as a priority were established early on, would less families end up dysfunctional?"[11] Indeed, when *relational time* is practiced as an ongoing part of family life, communication improves. And, based on observations of family practitioners cited by Jones, as families' communication progresses,

> "they: (a) share common experiences and interests from which they can draw upon to stimulate communication, (b) build enduring relationships, (c) foster a spirit of oneness and loyalty, (d) get to know each other as individuals, (e) learn to appreciate each other's strengths and understand the nature of weaknesses, (f) create intimate friendships due to time . . . building memories, (g) see themselves as part of a team that extends outside of the home, (h) learn more about the problems they face daily, and (i) define and practice family orals and legends."[12]

The importance of the practice of *relational time* also lies in the trust among family members that results. Indeed, as Jones states, without trust, "communication becomes exhausting, difficult, ineffective, and the messages become meaningless. The learning that occurs within the family is also difficult to replace. It is learning at its peak due to its informality and it is what will be relied upon when families face crises."[13]

Sacred Time

There is a kind of reckoning of time that embraces the holy. In this conceptualization of time, family members *remember* God's unceasing relationship with us; and we recognize that our home is a holy space and time apart from the church the clergyperson serves and in which the family participates. It is the space to *interpret* the nature and meaning of God's relationship with us and desire for our lives. We recognize that the parsonage is the church's house and there are times for the hospitable gathering of members. But, significantly, it is the clergy families' space and time not simply for *remembering* the nature of the Divine-human relationship in the family's life, but for *re-member-ing,* experientially, the bonds of family and *responding* to the trials and triumphs of the family.

Time is also reckoned as sacred to the extent that each moment of family life is cherished as time given by God to honor. In this sense, life takes on an improvisational character in which the family learns to lean into each successive moment "knowing" what *might happen,* but not "knowing" what *will happen* and *when*. Each moment is received as God's gift for family members to create, to improvise, and with which to proceed on the journey faithfully and imaginatively, as the spiritual says, "to see what the end will be."[14] This understanding of the improvisatory nature of sacred time conveys the notion that life is finite and that each moment, by its very nature, is comprised of unique, non-repeatable, non-retrievable moments, each with its own surprises, both good and bad. But, this kind of experience of time also entails a surrendering or relinquishment to God of a certain degree of control, resulting from the view that life is indeed given by God as gift.

This perspective of created time as sacred time opens the way for clergy, clergy families, and ecclesial head to see the unfolding nature of clergy family life in a new way. Life unfolds moment by moment as opportunity for clergy family members to share one another's stories, to reveal to one another the preciousness and the fragility of life as well as the need and opportunity for sharing compassion, and together, to face into the winds of promise that overtake the winds of challenge. Family life that is seen as gift from God also counters the view that building and nurturing family relationships *takes time*. Rather, the unfolding of this sacred time focuses on wholeness-producing relationships that *deserve time*–time to listen and self-disclose; time to simply be with one another; time to hold and time to let go; time to pray, and sing, and cry, and laugh, and shout, and dance; time to eat together; time to imagine life not yet revealed with willingness to move on with courage and hope. Indeed, when this happens, time is *lived* not simply in response to our embrace of God's gift, but in recognition of the temporal space where God has already come and where God remains the Holy Present One who becomes known in shared family relationships.

Creating or Re-creating Steps of Promise

A journey of promise for clergy families becomes possible as these families' address unique challenges of clergy family life. Again, we have suggested key processes for this to happen. But, concrete steps must be undertaken to ensure the opportunities for the families to engage in these processes. Steps are needed that guarantee occasions for what may be called "time talk." We have indicated that these processes may be carried out within individual clergy family units with or without a spiritual guide or pastoral caregiver; or the processes may be undertaken in small family groups or clusters as well as in workshops or retreats with the guidance of pastoral caregivers.

At the family level, it is important that families take the necessary steps to protect family time. Entering into the processes we have presented begins with this step. Protecting family time is also enhanced by other activities that draw family members together, such as family games, rituals, coming together at meal times, on vacations, having family meetings, and entering into both one-on-one and whole family conversations. This does not mean becoming time managers. It simply means creating relational time to be together that may require clergy and other family members to curtail the number of outside activities and reduce Internet and television time.[15]

An important second step should be taken at the congregational and denominational levels. It cannot be assumed that congregations know or understand fully the realities of clergy family life. Steps must be taken by denominations to disseminate information and recommendations that facilitate congregational awareness of and sensitivity to the needs of clergy families. Emphasis may be placed on family time including vacations and sabbaticals, the family's need to build a sense of home in the parsonage, and to decide the nature and extent of the role of family members in the life of the church.

Steps also must be taken to provide supports at the denominational level, including personnel and places to assist clergy families' engagement of the processes included in this resource. Further steps may include needs assessments that can reveal specific needs and interests of clergy families followed by intentional denominational responses to the findings. It is well, too, to monitor the extent of clergy time investment in meetings in light of what appears to be increasing requirements for clergy attendance at meetings at the congregational, regional, and denominational levels. In this regard, as with congregations, it is important that denominational leaders practice an awareness of and sensitivity to the need for specialized attention to the quality of life, relational time, and the cultivation of sacred time in clergy families.

Clearly, it will require continued intentional time and effort at the family, congregational, and denominational levels to enliven the promise of a generative future or a future with hope for clergy families. This effort is an essential one for clergy who serve in ministry and familial roles and for their families.

ENDNOTES

Prologue

1. The proverb is found in Julia Stewart, *African Proverbs and Wisdom* (Secaucus, NJ: Citadel Press, Carol Publishing Group, 1998), 150.
2. Findings of recent research on the effects of relocation in clergy families appears in: Marsha Wiggins Frame, "Relocation and Well-Being in United Methodist Clergy and Their Spouses: What Pastoral Counselors Need to Know," *Pastoral Psychology* 46(6), 1998:415-430; Michael Morris and Priscilla Blanton, "Predictors of Family Functioning Among Clergy and Spouses: Influences of Social Context and Perceptions of Work-Related Stressors," *Journal of Child and Family Studies* 7(1), 1998:27-41.
3. An insightful chapter entitled "Parsonages and Moving Vans," appears in the seminal work of David and Vera Mace. See: David & Vera Mace, *What's Happening to Clergy Marriages?* (Nashville: Abingdon, 1980), 72-79.
4. See Edward P. Wimberly, *Recalling Our Own Stories: The Spiritual Renewal of Religious Caregivers* (San Francisco: Jossey-Bass, 1997).
5. It is clear that seminary students today come with ideas and images of success measured in material terms and a desire to achieve success quickly. The pressures from ecclesiastical colleagues and superiors are explored in David & Vera Mace, *What's Happening in Clergy Marriages?*, 54-55. Also, the problems of the perfectionistic lifestyle are described in Michael Morris and Priscilla Blanton, "Predictors of Family Functioning Among Clergy and Spouses: Influences of Social Context and Perceptions of Work-Related Stressors," 39.
6. The situation of children in clergy families is detailed in research findings in Kimberly Sparrow Strange and Lori A Sheppard, "Evaluations of Clergy Children Versus Non-Clergy Children: Does a Negative Stereotype Exist?" *Pastoral Psychology* 50(1), September 2001:53-60; and C. Lee, *PKs: Helping Pastor's Kids Through Their Identity Crisis* (Grand Rapids: Zondervan, 1992).
7. Jack O. Balswick & Judith K. Balswick, *The Family: A Christian Perspective on the Contemporary Home,* Second edition (Grand Rapids: Baker Books, 1999), 352.
8. Gertrud Mueller Nelson, *To Dance With God: Family Ritual and Community Celebration* (New York: Paulist Press), 19.
9. J. Clinton McCann, Jr., "The Book of Psalms: Introduction, Commentary, and Reflections," in Leander E. Keck, et.al., editors, *The New Interpreter's Bible: A*

Commentary in Twelve Volumes, Volume IV (Nashville: Abingdon, 1996), 1118.
10. *Ibid.*
11. *Ibid.*
12. Joan D. Chittister, *Scarred by Struggle, Transformed by Hope* (Grand Rapids: William B. Eerdmans, 2003), 83.

Chapter One

1. See Don Friesen, "Stirrings in the Mind's Deep Caves," An Ottawa Mennonite Church Sermon, recorded in:
   http://www.ottawamennonite.ca/sermons/caves.htm
2. *Ibid.*
3. Howard John Clinebell, *Intimate Marriage* (New York: HarperCollins College Division, 1970).
4. For details related to the following questions, see: D. Jean Clandinin and P. Michael Connelly, *Narrative Inquiry: Experience and Story in Qualitative Research* (San Francisco: Jossey-Bass, 2000), 11.
5. A version of the song appears in *Songs of Zion* (Nashville: Abingdon, 1991), #83.
6. See Edward P. Wimberly, *Recalling Our Own Stories: The Spiritual Renewal of Religious Caregivers* (San Francisco: Jossey-Bass, 2000).
7. E. Brooks Holifield, "The Hero and the Minister in American Culture," *Theology Today,* (January 1977):373-376.

Chapter Two

1. This editor's note appears in Colin Greer & Herbert Kohl, et. al., *A Call to Character: A Family Treasury* (New York: HarperCollins, 1995), 333.
2. In their publication, Charles Foster and his colleagues affirm that "Congregations—and the public—have high and consistent expectations for the quality and character of the clergy's public work." Our position here is that this reality in the lives of clergy extends to clergy family members. See Charles Foster, et. al., *Educating Clergy: Teaching Practices and Pastoral Imagination* (San Francisco: Jossey-Bass, 2005), 157.
3. *Ibid.,* 156.
4. Edward P. Wimberly, *Recalling Our Own Stories,* 6-8.

Chapter Three

1. Rachel Naomi Remen, M.D., *Kitchen Table Wisdom: Stories That Heal* (New York: Riverhead Books, 1996), 185.
2. Robert Kohler and Mary Ann Moman, "Commentary: Itinerancy, a Strategy for the Church's Mission," A United Methodist News Service Article, July 2007. Website: http://www.wfn.org/2001/07/msg00020.html
3. Betty Carter and Monica McGoldrick, *The Changing Family Life Cycle: A Framework for Family Therapy* (Boston: Allyn and Bacon, 1989), 143.

Chapter Four

1. See Babu Ayindo, Sam Gbaydee Doe, and Janice Jenner, *When You Are a Peacebuilder: Stories and Reflections on Peacebuilding from Africa* (Harrisburg, PA: Eastern Mennonite University, 2001), 12. The resource is also available on the website: http://www.emu.edu/ctp/janwhen.pdf
2. For a discussion of nodal and life cycle transition, see Edward P. Wimberly, *Counseling African American Marriages and Families* (Louisville: Westminster John Knox, 1997), 51-64.
3. Sylvia Ann Hewlett and Cornel West, *The War Against Parents: What We Can Do for America's Beleaguered Moms and Dads* (New York: Houghton Mifflin Company, 1998), 26-53.
4. *Ibid.*, 28.
5. *Ibid.*, 30.

Chapter Five

1. Joan D. Chittister, *Scarred by Struggle, Transformed by Hope*, 13.
2. The discussion appears in Brooks Holifield, "The Hero and the Minister in American Culture, 371-379.
3. See David and Vera Mace, *What's Happening to Clergy Marriages?*
4. Carrie Doehring, *Taking Care: Monitoring Power Dynamics and Relational Boundaries in Pastoral Counseling* (Nashville: Abingdon, 1995), 80.
5. Charles V. Gerkin proposes a practical model of interpretation for use by pastors in confronting common human situations of individuals, family members and parish communities. This model includes a phase that emphasizes what Gerkin calls "interpretive judgment." The concept refers to action directed toward desired outcomes. See Charles V. Gerkin, "Interpretation and Hermeneutics, Pastoral," in Rodney J. Hunter, General Editor, *Dictionary of Pastoral Care and Counseling* (Nashville: Abingdon, 1990), 592-593.
6. The definition is built on the work of Edwin H. Friedman, *Generation to Generation: Family Process in Church and Synagogue* (New York: Guilford Press, 1985), 208-210.
7. *Ibid.*
8. *Ibid.*
9. Murray Bowen, *Family Therapy in Clinical Practice* (New York: Jason Aronson, 1978), 539-543.

Chapter Six

1. Rachel Naomi Remen, M.D., *Kitchen Table Wisdom*, 110.
2. D. Jean Clandinin and F. Michael Connelly, *Narrative Inquiry*, xxxi.
3. Colin Murray Parks, "Disaster, Public," in Rodney J. Hunter, General Editor, *Dictionary of Pastoral Care and Counseling* (Nashville: Abingdon, 1990), 285.
4. *Ibid.*
5. *Ibid.*

6. See Gerard Egan, *The Skilled Helper: A Problem-Management Approach to Helping* (Pacific Grove, CA: Brooks/Cole, 1998), 128-129.

7. *Ibid.*, 130-131.

8. The opportunity-finding questions included are part of a longer list provided in Egan, *The Skilled Helper*, 132.

9. Egan identifies fear of intensity, lack of trust, shame, fear of disorganization, and fear of change as forms of reluctance and resistance that can emerge in story-sharing aimed toward helping. See Egan, 138-139.

10. Egan is helpful in his presentation of skills of attending, listening, and understanding. See Egan, 61-79.

Epilogue

1. Jetse Sprey, "Time Bound," In Kerry J. Daly, ed., *Minding the Time in Family Experience: Emerging Perspectives and Issues*, 37-57. (New York: Elsevier Science Ltd., 2001), 56.

2. Anne Streaty Wimberly, "Creating Time," *Circuit Rider*, 26(1), January-February 2002:16-17.

3. John R. Gillis, "Never Enough Time: Some Paradoxes of Modern Family Time(s)," In Kerry J. Daly, ed., *Minding the Time in Family Experience: Emerging Perspectives and Issues*, 19-36 (New York: Elsevier Science Ltd., 2001), 19.

4. *Ibid.*, 29.

5. See *Ibid.*, 29-30.

6. Gertrud Mueller Nelson, *To Dance With God: Family Ritual and Community Celebration* (New York: Paulist Press), 19.

7. Kim McGarraugh Jones, "Protecting and Enhancing Family Time: Challenges, Strategies, and Implications for Family Life Educators," In Kerry J. Daly, ed., *Minding the Time in Family Experience: Emerging Perspectives and Issues*, 403-421 (New York: Elsevier Science Ltd., 2001), 406.

8. Hendricks uses the term, "generative futures," to convey the kind of future that is seen as more than one's own, but rather on what is entered on behalf of others. See Jon Hendricks, "It's About Time," In Susan H. McFadden and Robert C. Atchley, eds., *Aging and the Meaning of Time: A Multidisciplinary Exploration*, 21-50 (New York: Springer, 2001), 42.

9. The concept and description of relational time is presented in: Anne Streaty Wimberly, "Creating Time," 16-17; and Anne Streaty Wimberly, "Acknowledging the Gift of Time," *Opening Article, These Moments: Claiming Time for Spiritual Growth, Presbyterian Church (PCUSA) Devotional Guide*, January-March, 2003:1.

10. Jones, "Protecting and Enhancing Family Time," 410.

11. *Ibid.*

12. *Ibid.*

13. *Ibid.*

14. A version of the words to the song appear in: John Lovell, Jr., Black Song: *The Forge and the Flame, The Story of How the Afro-American Spiritual Was Hammered Out* (New York: The Macmillan Company, 1972), 323, 379.

15. Jones, "Protecting and Enhancing Family Time," 411.

BIBLIOGRAPHY

Ayindo, Babu; Doe, Sam Gbaydee; and Jenner, Janice. *When You Are a Peacebuilder: Stories and Reflections on Peacebuilding from Africa.* Harrisburg: Eastern Mennonite University, 2001. Website: http://www.emu.edu/ctp/janwhen.pdf

Balswick, Jack O. & Balswick, Judith K. *The Family: A Christian Perspective on the Contemporary Home.* Second edition. Grand Rapids: Baker Books, 1999.

Bowen, Murray. *Family Therapy in Clinical Practice.* New York: Jason Aronson, 1978.

Chittister, Joan D. *Scarred by Struggle, Transformed by Hope.* Grand Rapids: Wm. B. Eerdmans, 2003.

Carter, Betty and McGoldrick, Monica. *The Changing Life Cycle: A Framework for Family Therapy.* Boston: Allyn and Bacon, 1989.

Clandinin, D. Jean and Connelly, P. Michael. *Narrative Inquiry: Experience and Story in Qualitative Research.* San Francisco: Jossey-Bass, 2000.

Clinebell, Howard John. *The Intimate Marriage.* New York: HarperCollins College Division, 1970.

Daly, Kerry J. Ed. *Minding the Time in Family Experience: Emerging Perspectives and Issues.* New York: Elsevier Science Ltd., 2001.

Doerhring, Carrie. *Taking Care: Monitoring Power Dynamics and Relational Boundaries in Pastoral Counseling.* Nashville: Abingdon, 1995.

Egan, Gerard. *The Skilled Helper: A Problem-Management Approach to Helping.* Pacific Grove, Ca: Brooks/Cole, 1998.

Foster, Charles R. et. al. *Educating Clergy: Teaching Practices and Pastoral Imagination.* San Francisco: Jossey-Bass, 2005.

Frame, Marsha Wiggins. "Relocation and Well-Being in United Methodist Clergy and Their Spouses: What Pastoral Counselors Need to Know," *Pastoral Psychology* 46(6), 1998:415-430.

Friedman, Edwin H. *Generation to Generation: Family Process in Church and Synagogue.* New York: Guilford, 1985.

Friesen, Don. "Stirrings in the Mind's Deep Caves." An Ottawa Mennonite Church Sermon. Website: http://www.ottawamennonite.ca/sermons/caves.htm

Gerkin, Charles V. "Interpretation and Hermeneutics, Pastoral." In Rodney J. Hunter, General Ed. *Dictionary of Pastoral Care and Counseling.* Nashville: Abingdon, 1990.

Gillis, John R. "Never Enough Time: Some Paradoxes of Modern Family Time(s)," In Kerry J. Daly, Ed., *Minding the Time in Family Experience: Emerging Perspectives and Issues,* 19-36. New York: Elsevier Science Ltd., 2001.

Greer, Colin and Kohl, Herbert, et. Al. *A Call to Character: A Family Treasury.* New York: HarperCollins, 1995.

Hendricks, Jon. "It's About Time." In Susan H. McFadden and Robert C. Atchley, Eds. *Aging and the Meaning of Time: A Multidisciplinary Exploration,* 21-50. New York: Springer, 2001.

Hewlett, Sylvia Ann and West, Cornel. *The War Against Parents: What We Can Do for America's Beleaguered Moms and Dads.* New York: Houghton Mifflin, 1998.

Holifield, E. Brooks. "The Hero and the Minister in American Culture. *Theology Today,* January 1977):373-376.

Jones, Kim McGarraugh. "Protecting and Enhancing Family Time: Challenges, Strategies, and Implications for Family Life Educators." In Kerry J. Daly, Ed., *Minding the Time in Family Experience: Emerging Perspectives and Issues,* 403-421. New York: Elsevier Science Ltd., 2001.

Kohler, Robert and Moman, Mary Ann. "Commentary: Itinerancy a Strategy for Church's Mission." A United Methodist News Service Article, July 2007. Website: http://www.wfn.org/2001/07/msg00020.html

Lee, C. *Pks: Helping Pastors' Kids Through Their Identity Crisis.* Grand Rapids: Zondervan, 1992.

Lovell, John, Jr. *Black Song: The Forge and the Flame, The Story of How the Afro-American Spiritual Was Hammered Out.* New York: The Macmillan Company, 1972.

Mace, David and Vera. *What's Happening to Clergy Marriages?* Nashville: Abingdon, 1980.

McCann, J. Clinton, Jr. "The Book of Psalms: Introduction, Commentary, and Reflections." In Leander E. Keck, et. al., editors, *The New Interpreter's Bible: A Commentary in Twelve Volumes, Volume IV.* Nashville: Abingdon, 1996.

Morris, Michael and Blanton, Priscilla. "Predictors of Family Functioning Among Clergy and Spouses: Influences of Social Context and Perceptions of Work-Related Stressors," *Journal of Child and Family Studies* 7(1), 1998:27-41.

Nelson, Gertrud Mueller. *To Dance With God: Family Ritual and Community Celebration.* New York: Paulist Press), 19.

Parks, Colin Murray. "Disaster, Public." In Rodney J. Hunter, General Ed. *Dictionary of Pastoral Care and Counseling.* Nashville: Abingdon, 1990._

Remen, Rachel Naomi, M.D. *Kitchen Table Wisdom: Stories That Heal.* New York: Riverhead Books, 1996.

Songs of Zion. Nashville: Abingdon, 1991.

Sprey, Jetse. "Time Bound," In Kerry J. Daly, ed. *Minding the Time in Family Experience: Emerging Perspectives and Issues*, 37-57. New York: Elsevier Science Ltd., 2001.

Stewart, Julia. *African Proverbs and Wisdom*. Secaucus, NJ: Citadel Press, Carol Publishing Group, 1998.

Strange, Kimberly Sparrow and Sheppard, Lori. "Evaluations of Clergy Children Versus Non-Clergy Children: Does a Negative Stereotype Exist?" *Pastoral Psychology* 50(1), September 2001:53-60.

Wimberly, Anne Streaty. "Creating Time," *Circuit Rider* 26(1), January-February 2002:16-17.

_____. "Acknowledging the Gift of Time," Opening Article, *These Moments: Claiming Time for Spiritual Growth*, Presbyterian Church (PCUSA) Devotional Guide, January-March, 2003:1.

Wimberly, Edward P. *Counseling African American Marriages and Families*. Louisville: Westminster John Knox, 1997.

_____. *Recalling Our Own Stories: The Spiritual Renewal of Religious Caregivers*. San Francisco: Jossey-Bass, 1997.